A HISTORY OF POLITICAL THOUGHT

A HISTORY OF POLITICAL THOUGHT

N. JAYAPALAN

ATLANTIC PUBLISHERS AND DISTRIBUTORS

Published by
ATLANTIC PUBLISHERS AND DISTRIBUTORS
B-2, Vishal Enclave, New Delhi-110 027
Phones 5413460, 5429987

Sales Office
4346/4C, Ansari Road, Darya Ganj,
New Delhi-110 002
Phones 3273880, 3285873, 3280451
Fax 91-11-3285873

ISBN 81-7156-689-8

Typeset at
APD Computer Graphics, Delhi
Printed in India at
Mehra Offset Press, New Delhi-110 002

Preface

A History of Political Thought provides us a detailed study about various political thinkers of various periods. Their life and thought will prove to be more useful to the students of today. The students of today are the statesman and administrators of tomorrow. Therefore, it is imperative for them to be thoroughly conversant with political thought.

I have written this book primarily to meet the requirements of the students preparing for B.A. (Hons.), M.A. and competitive examinations. Almost all important points have been discussed. The style is lucid and simple as to easily fall within the grasp of even moderate students. I hope that the present book will prove to be more useful to the students than any other book on the subject available in the market. I also hope that the book will serve as a textbook.

I wish to pay my sincere thanks to my publishers for their whole hearted cooperation in completing this book.

Suggestions for the improvement of the book in the subsequent editions will be highly appreciated.

N. JAYAPALAN

Preface

A History of Political Thought provides us a detailed study about various political thinkers of various periods. Their life and thought will prove to be more useful to the students of History, the students of today, are the statesman and administrators of tomorrow. Therefore, it is imperative for them to be thoroughly conversant with political thought.

I have written this book primarily to meet the requirements of the students preparing for B.A. (Hons.), M.A. and competitive examinations. Almost all important points have been discussed. The style is lucid and simple as to easily fall within the grasp of even moderate students. I hope that the present book will prove to be more useful to the students than any other book on the subject available in the market. I also hope that the book will serve as a textbook.

I wish to pay my sincere thanks to my publishers for their whole-hearted cooperation in completing this [illegible].

Suggestions for the improvement of the book in its subsequent editions will be highly appreciated.

N. JAYAPALAN

CONTENTS

I

Thomas Hobbes (1588–1679)

Thomas Hobbes was an English man who lived during the time of Charles II. He was born at Westport in North Wilts in 1588, the year of Spanish Armada. During this time Hobbes said, his mother gave birth to twins-himself and fear. His father was a vicar who later on deserted his wife and three children. When Hobbes was very young he learned Greek and Latin. He was educated at Malmesbury and then at Oxford. On leaving the Oxford University he became tutor to the heir of William Cavendish later Earl of Devenshire. This association or connection facilitated him to meet many leading figures of his day such as Ben Jonson, Bacon, Clarendon, Harvey and Galileo.

Thomas Hobbes was a man of very studious nature. This enabled him to become a classical scholar. At the age of forty he turned to philosophy by way of mathematics. As a result he published his first work of translation of Thucydides. He published his "De Live" in 1642 and the "Elements of Law" in 1650. With the outbreak of the Civil War, he removed to Paris. Here he became tutor to Charles II for sometime. His masterpiece the "Leviathan" was published in 1651 while he was in Paris. The following year he was back in Protectorate England and published "Decorpove Politico" in 1655 and "De Homine" in 1659.

Thomas Hobbes was the first Englishman who wrote comprehensively on political Philosophy. His most famous work the "Leviathan" was severely and seriously criticised by contemporary writers as expected by Hobbes Whitehall found Leviathan "as full of damnable opinions as a toad is of Poison" "a rebels" "catechism" and "good doctrine of a popish cabal." According to Bramhill it would "put all to fire and flame."

His view of man : The political philosophy of Hobbes is based on scientific materialism which he grasped from the system of motion of Galileo and Newton. According to C.L. Wayper "The Universe for Hobbes, is a machine a machine made up of particles moving according to a mechanical law which he believes that Galileo has shown can be determined." This movement or motion as he calls it, is the very principal of universe. He further adds that man is a microcosm an epitome of the great universe. He also is a machine more complicated than plants or beasts but composed as they are and as the universe is of moving particles. In accordance with his materialistic principles reality consists always in the motion of bodies which is "transmitted through the sense organs of central nervous system where it appears as sensation." Sense organs like eyes, ears, etc., are essential for motion. "Man's receptive powers like memory, imagination and prudence are the cumulative results of sensation. From these motion produces active powers *viz*. emotions or passions.

According to Hobbes appetites or aversions are either born with man or acquired in due course of time. The object of man's appetite is called "good" and that of his aversion is called "evil". Good or evil depends upon human feelings towards it. It may also differ with individual and individual. When he gets what he wills he is said to enjoy Felicity. Felicity is not an end in itself and it gives place for endless desire. Thus life is "a perpetual and restless desire of power after power that ceaseth only in death". For "man cannot assure the power and means to live well which he has present, without the acquisition of more." From this it is obvious that the individual described by Hobbes is completely self-centred.

According to Hobbes every single man is an absolutely solitary individual, contrasting men with bees and ants he said "Men are continually in competition for honour and dignity, which these creatures are not, consequently amongst men, there ariseth on the ground envy and hatred and finally war." He further said that since knowledge comes from the senses and different senses cannot see the same world, a man and his world must be one of different from the world of other man. Different individuals have absolutely separate worlds, separate pleasures, truths, goods and they belong to no order, moral or politic. Hence, Wayper says that Hobbes "is perhaps the greatest individualist in the history of political thought. He is an extreme doctrine of individualism embracing everything."

The individual of Hobbes has the possibility of breaking down his solitude since he has the power of speech. Language enables him to give way to his thoughts. Then it is possible for him to define, to argue and to reason. For Hobbes reason is "nothing but reckoning that is adding and subtracting of the consequences of general names agreed upon for the marking and signifying of our thoughts." It is this reason together with religion that distinguishes man from the brute. Reason is artificial the passions are natural. Reason may help man in his search for happiness. He has to overcome certain difficulties on the way. Thesc difficulties are due to his environment and also to like defect in his own character.

All men are equal by nature in mind and body. Most people think that they are wiser than others. Man lives in this state of nature. Neither right or wrong, justice nor injustice, have place in it. Force and fraud are its important virtues. In this connection Hobbes says that there is no place for industry. In such a condition man's vain glory or pride makes him unfit for success; but the condition itself is the result not of his defects but of his very nature. The state of nature, as Hobbes sees it is the ill condition which man by mere nature is actually place in." From this condition he wants to extricate that man.

His view of the state : Hobbes has given a very good account about the state in his monumental work "Leviathan" Reason teaches men to obey Natural Laws. According to him, they are nineteen in number. According to the First Law of Nature that every man should seek peace and preserve it. Without peace he will not find Felicity. If he cannot obtain peace he should use all helps and advantages of war. The Second Law of Nature lays down that a man must be willing along with others and in the interest of peace and self-preservation, to forswear his right to all things be contact with as much liberty as would allow others over himself and transfer some of his rights by a contract. The Third Law of Nature says that "men perform their covenants made."

The Fourth Law of Nature describes that the man to whom the rights are transferred causes no injury to the one who makes that transfer. Other Laws of Nature deal about the spirit of freedom, sense of equity etc.

Two things are very important in Hobbes's Natural Laws. Wayper says that the Natural Laws of Hobbes are not Natural Laws as commonly understood. The tradition of Natural Law goes back to the stoics. It has been identified with perfect Morality or Eternal Justice. The actual law is the imperfect reflection. But Hobbe's Natural Laws are merely "Counsels of prudence". These laws are necessary to fulfil each and every individual good. Thus the Laws of Nature serve as the supreme basis of society and later on of government.

The Social Contract : Hobbes has given a beautiful pen picture about the social contract in his famous book Leviathan. He was the first political thinker to propound a precise and explicit theory of social contract. He describes about the pre-social side of human nature. The human beings are selfish and egoistic. They have no sense of right and wrong. They do not know pity and compassion. Even then they feel fear, distrust and suspection. They realise the need to form a civil society enter into a contract among themselves. As a result of the contract are born the state and government.

Will, finally enables men to take the action to form a society. The need is a "will not to will." It means one accepts a limitation on one's will and does not always insist on one's will. This is carried out by way of a contract. According to this contract all men agree to transfer their rights to a third party agreed upon. The third party is the representative of all the men. At this juncture every man says in the following manner, "I authorise and give up my right of governing myself to this man, or this assembly of men, on this condition, that thou give up thy right to him, and authorise all his actions in like manner."

Such a contract must be perpetual and irrevocable. It is based on fear. Hence it is contrary to man's instincts. Moreover men are notorious backsliders. To make this covenant very strong and everlasting the representative is given common power to rule the common people. The recipient of such power or the third party according to Hobbes should be a king. Like all men he may be selfish and however the self-indulgence one will be cheaper than the self-indulgence of many. It is thus clear that this Leviathan possesses absolute power because he himself is not a party to the contract. He stands for strong state. But it is not the case in democracy and aristocracy. The rulers in those forms of governments are after power. Hobbes does not necessarily support such royal absolutism. His is a doctrine of the absolute state, not of the absolute kind.

Sovereignty : The sovereign of Hobbes is the sole and whole source of laws. Of course he is the sole interpreter of laws. He is not subject to civil laws. Wayper points out that Leviathan is the creator Right and Justice. Therefore, his laws can never be unjust or immoral. The commands of the sovereign are called laws. Indeed, there is only one limitation to the powers of the kind *i.e.* he cannot command a man to himself. The kind is also the sole interpreter of the laws of God. If Leviathan fails to protect, men are then back in the state of nature and free to obey a de facto monarch.

There is liberty under Leviathan. It is that which man enjoys in the silence of the laws Leviathan has no passion for undue interference. Men can expect the liberty "to buy and sell and otherwise contract with one another to choose their own abode, their own diet, their own trade of life and institute their children as they themselves fit and the like." In addition to this Leviathan cannot force "man to believe" "Thought is free" to all. From this it is clear that his political philosophy was quite individualistic in essence as against his theory of absolute sovereign.

The sovereign has the right of hearing and deciding all controversial questions which may arise concerning laws. He is the person one who is responsible for official authority. He has the power of conferring honours and privileges for service to the state. Thus, the sovereign possesses absolute inalienable indivisible and unlimited powers.

■■

II

Benedict Spinoza (1632–1677)

Benedictus de Spinoza was born to Jewish parents in Amsterdam (Holland) in 1632. During the revolt of the Netherlands against Spain, he came to Holland. His studies had been mainly Jewish, but he was an independent thinker. He acquired sufficient knowledge in his Jewish studies to wean him away from orthodox theology. He followed the main principles of Descarte. "I think therefore I am" the dictum of Descarte greatly influenced him.

Spinoza's contributions are : (1) Ethics Geometrically Demonstrated, (2) On the Improvement of the Intellect, (3) The Principles of Cartesian Philosophy, (4) Theologico-Political Treatise, (5) Political Treatise, and (6) Treatise on the Rainbow.

Though Spinoza followed the fundamental ideas of Descarte's Physics, he indicated three distinct features in Cartesian metaphysics. Those three features were unsatisfactory to him. The were : (1) transcendence of God, (2) the substantial dualism of mind, and (3) the ascription of free will as liberilm arbitrium both to God and to human beings. According to him those doctrines made the world unintelligible. He believes that it is possible to construct a system of metaphysics which would be intelligible. One of the main motives in the construction of Spinoza's system was deep religious feeling.

According to Spinoza God is a conscious thing; really it is an omniscient being, but without free will and purposes. He acts according to the necessity of His own nature. Some people may be good; some may be bad. It does not mean that God should have special care for those people on the basis of their likes and dislikes. All things in Nature are determined by necessity. He argues that all events and man's actions are determined, by their proper course and are just not accidental or providential. God and universe are identical things. He too observes certain necessary laws in the matts. From this it is clear that his system is based on universal determinism and not on fatalism. In this connection he describes about the importance of knowledge. He defines that the mental correlate for physical action is called knowledge. There are three types of knowledge according to Spinoza *viz.* opinion or imagination, reason and intuition.

Another feature of his ethico-political system is the denial of human free will. The will and the understanding are one and the same. Man is free in so far as his emotions are active rather than passive. To attain Freedom reason must regulate passions. According to him, the natural man is strictly presocial as revealed by Hobbes. Men who are good by reason seek useful things to them and they desire nothing for themselves which they do not desire for the rest of mankind. It is thus crystal clear that his ethics is not based on egoism but on altruistic utilitarianism.

After giving a graphic picture about his ethical foundations of political order, he sets forth his idea of defence of democracy in his monumental works. According to him, the philosopher must study human passions and their modifications exactly as if they were properties of atmosphere. But he must also consider the practical side of politics from the human view point. It is found in the Theologico-Political Treatise rather than in the political treatise. From the above works we know about monarchy, aristocracy and democracy with an emphasis upon positive laws and institutions.

In Spinoza's state of nature men lived in accordance with their natural instinctive self-preservation. Active emotion (Reason) was very essential for man. If this was predominant in man there would be no conflict. Hence, no civil authority or government would be necessary. But majority of men are governed by passive desires leading to conflict for possession and properties. Hence, in the state of nature might was right. In the state of nature the individuals surrender their power to a sovereign authority for the sake of enhancing each man's power of self-preservation. Thus, the civil society comes into existence as the result of a common agreement by those individuals. Here, the might of the whole limits the might of the individual. The sovereign authority is for general welfare. He regulates the interest of the people by means of good laws. Law is the epitome of reason and its objective is enlarge the scope of freedom and happiness, stability and security and peace and order. Philosophy is the ultimate end of the state. For the preservation of piety and public peace "freedom of philosophizing" is necessary. It is seen from his Theologico-political treatise. He disregards monarchy and favours democracy since it limits the right of the chief magistrates. According to him "democracy" does not indicate the number of voters from whom the office holders are chosen, but rather that there are laws which specifically determine who will be eligible to vote. He further says that a viable democratic government is based upon consent and co-operation but is run by the rational men, and governed by just laws towards the end-philosophic freedom.

Spinoza puts great stress on the necessity of religion to obtain the best republic. Religion must be purified for the same. He considered Bible as a compendium of practical and precise social and moral law and as a code of behaviour. His object was to avoid subjecting the state to the diverse judgement and passions of everyone. For that purpose he remarked that the clergymen should not be given political power because it tends to corrupt them. Naturally, it will affect both the church and the state. According to him, religious functions must be separated from political functions and sovereign is entitled to decide wheather a particular thing is lawful or not.

Hence, Spinoza's political philosophy is very significant. He is the first and foremost man to write about the systematic defence of democracy.

■■

III

John Locke (1632–1704)

John Locke is considered as the greatest figure in the history of English political thought. He was born in 1632 at Wrington in Somerset Shire to Puritan parents. His father was a lawyer who served in the Parliamentary Army during the Civil war. He had his early education at Westminster. Then he had his education in Christ Church College at Oxford. He took great interest in philosophy and science. He also studied medicine, but never took his medical degree. The writings of Descartes awakened his interest in philosophy and his friendship with Robert Boyle aroused his enthusiasm for the natural sciences. The medical knowledge of Locke created a chance to meet Lord Ashley, the leader of the Whig party in 1666. He saved his life by a skilful operation. Later on, he was appointed confidential secretary to Lord Shaftesbury (Lord Ashley). This association with Shaftesbury was to influence Locke's life just as his connection with Devonshires had influenced Hobbes. In 1696, he became Commissioner to the Board of Trade and Plantations. He died in the year 1704 in Essex.

In 1689 Locke published his first "Letter concerning Toleration" in Latin. In the same year he published the English version for the same. His greatest work the "Essay Concerning Human Understanding" was published in 1690. The two "Treatises of Civil Government" were also published in the same year. His other works were "Second Letter on Toleration", "Third Letter on Toleration", "Some thoughts concerning Education" and his fourth and final work was "Letter on Toleration".

Locke's View of Human Nature : Locke has not given a very clear picture of human nature as Hobbes has given in the Leviathan.

His ideas in this regard can be seen in the second treatise. Further his view of man is summed up in his "Essay on Human Understanding." Like Hobbes, Locke also says that all men are born equal. According to Locke desire is the spring of all human action. It is a feeling of uneasiness. It is identified with pain, a feeling of which men want to rid themselves. The aim of all human action is to substitute pleasure for pain. Bentham another political philosopher has also given the same picture about the human nature. He called this as "Psychological egoistic hedonism." Hence Locke says, "what has an aptness to produce pleasure in us is what we call good, and what is apt to produce pain in us we call evil."

Further Locke describes about theory of morals in his "Essay on Human Understanding". History shows clearly, he says that the morality of one society is the immorality of another. Locke repeatedly has stated in his three chapters that morals like mathematics is a demonstrable science subject to ascertainable universal laws, but he did not develop this idea so fully as could be wished.

Now Locke turns his attention to Bay something about these universal laws. They are the Divine Law and the National Laws. The Divine Law is God's will for man's behaviour. It is made available to man both by divine revelation and by the use of his own reason, and which is above all, to be looked for in the New Testament. The Natural Law is an eternal law, the criterion of good and evil, discoverable by reasoning and commanding men carry out the will of God.

It is obvious that Locke's view of human nature is not so profound and as consistent as that of Hobbes. His problem however is very much the same as that of Hobbes. Why do such men as his wish to form civil society? How can they do so? Locke's answer to the problem seems to be very different from Hobbes. Hobbes gave these ideas even before the event of the Glorious Revolution of 1688, a revolution which Hobbes would have regarded an anarchic and deplorable in the extreme.

Hobbes considers man as a brute and a creature of nature.

Locke considers that man is a member of a moral order and is subject to natural law. The man of Hobbes is always selfish whereas the man of Locke sometimes possesses helping tendency. Hence, the state of Locke is different from that of Hobbes. Naturally, men are very humane in their character. As a result they live in peace and harmony with each other. They can able to live without a state. According to Hobbes, man's life without a state would be miserable and dangerous. Sovereign is not responsible for his deeds. Contrarily Locke's state is established not because people need the same but because they require some convenience and comfort to acquire better and fitter life. There the sovereign is limited by the same moral order.

The State of Nature: According to Locke, the state of nature is a state in which men are equal and free. Thc state of nature is one of perfect freedom and of equality. Men are equal and free to act "as they think fit, within the bounds of Law of Nature." But it is not a state of licence. "The State of Nature has a Law of Nature to govern it, which obliges every one, and reason which is that law, teaches all mankind who will but consult it, that being all equal and independent, no one ought to harm another in his life, health, liberty or passions" ....according to Locke. From this Natural Law he derives certain natural rights like right to life, right to liberty and right to property. "Natural Law not only accords man rights it imposed duties upon him" the view given by Wayper is to be equated in this connection.

Locke does not equate the state of nature and war as Hobbes did in his Leviathan. A state of war is the view of Hobbes in which life is normally solitary, poor, nasty brutish and short. There is no peace. It is constantly upset by the corruption and viciousness of degenerate men. If men try to maintain their own rights by destroying others' rights there would be state of War. Locke has given clear cut differences between the state of nature and the state of war. But Hobbes shows no difference at all.

Moreover, Locke speaks of three essential wants in the state of nature. They are : (1) want of an established settled known law,

(2) want of a known and independent judge with authority to determine all differences according to the established law, and (3) the want of an executive power to enforce just decisions.

The Social Contract : John Locke was another English political philosopher who lived during the time of James II. During the time of James II Glorious Revolution broke out in England in 1688. Having witnessed the happenings of the Revolution he gave his theory of social contract in his "Two Treatises of Government" published in 1690. He championed the cause of limited monarchy in England. He stresses the words "in the consent of the people" in his theory.

Locke also started his theory with the idea of state of nature. But it differed from that of Hobbes. The state of nature of Hobbes was both pre-social and pre-political whereas Locke's was pre-political. The people of Locke had certain rights over life and property. At the same time there was no peace in the society. In order to escape from the evils they made a contract after surrendering their individual rights. By this contract state and sovereign came into existence. The sovereign was a party to the contract. He was responsible for his acts. The sovereign therefore, could not as Hobbes said be unlimited. With the consent of the people he did his governmental activities. If he violated the contract, he could be deposed. The people could resume their original liberty and establish a new form of government.

It was a contract which once made was irrevocable. It was a contract to which each generation must consent. According to Hobbes, the government should possess absolute power as a result of the social contracts. But Locke holds that the contract does not remove the supreme power from the people. The supreme power continue to remain with the people.

The State–Its form and Its characteristics : According to Locke, there are three wants in the state of nature. They are a known law, a known judge and a certain executive power. In addition to this he points out three remedies for the same viz. Legislative, judicial and executive powers. Locke calls the legislative power the first among them, "the supreme powers of the commonwealth." Secondly, there is the executive which includes the judicial power. The legislature need not always be in session, but the executive must be. It must always be on duty. Hence, these two powers must be separated. Here Locke shows his signal for the theory of separation of powers. In enunciating the doctrine of the separation of powers Locke was a foreigner to Montesquieu. It was the latter, however who classified powers into executive, legislative and judicial.

The third power that Locke points out is the federative power. This power enables the state to make treaties i.e. it is concerned with the state's external relations. However, he does not elaborate the same. But he shows too much importance to for formulation, execution and control of foreign policy.

Of these three powers the legislative not only the supreme power of the commonwealth, but sacred and unalterable in the hands where the community have once placed it. Here Locke is influenced by the experience of the English Revolution in which parliament asserted its supremacy.

The first and foremost characteristic of Locke's state is that it exists for the people who form it, they do not exist for it. Now and then he insists that "the end of government" is "the good of the community." He further points out that all true states must be founded on consent. The true state must be a constitutional state in which men acknowledge the rule of law. If a man is subject to the inconstant, uncertain, unknown, arbitrary will of another man, there can be no political liberty. So Government must possess discretionary and emergency powers. Another important characteristic of Locke's true state is that it is limited. It is not absolute. It is limited because it derives power from the people.

The State therefore should exist for the good of the people. It must depend on their consent. It should be constitutional and limited in its authority. If it acts otherwise it can be legitimately overthrown by means of revolution. But revolutions are not to be carried out by minority which would mean "Liberty for ambitious men to pull down well framed constitutions that out of their ruins they may build themselves fortunes."

Regarding Locke's state, Wayper points out three more

characteristics. It is a tolerant state which will respect differences of opinion. It is a negative state which does not seek to improve the character of its citizens or not to manage their lives, but which merely strives to secure their independence. It is the duty of the state to transform the selfish interest into public good. Then only people could be said to have entered civil society.

Theory of Property : The Right to property is one of the natural rights that existed in the state of nature. Locke attaches much importance to that of property. During the state of nature many differences arose over that property. These differences were the underlying causes for the war. Political thinkers have given their views regarding the importance of property. They have argued that it is the state which gives a legal and ethical status to property According to some it is a benefit from the organisation of state for other the state gives sanctions for the forceful taking of possessions from the common lot.

The concept of property had its foundation in Aristotle. Locke's theory begins ith the justification of property. He says that the earth was the gift of God and all therein for the support and comfort of all people. People must enjoy the truths of the earth. Every individual should use the earth for their benefit. So there are collective common ownership and individual use. Labour is also very essential to create property according to Locke.

The value of property is determined by man's labour. According to him, "As much land as a man tills, plants, improve, cultivates and can use the product of so much is his property." Further he stresses about the social benefit of cultivation. Hence earth is not valuable; but the labour of the people is valuable. Then the people created certain laws of property by consent after surrendering their primitive right. Afterwards Government establishes the rights of property and the laws governing their exercise. It is thus known to us that his purpose was to justify individual property as a fundamental right.

Later on his theory of property was used in defence of capitalism. It has become a tool for socialists to attack capitalism. According to capitalists property was a natural right and hence must be protected. But the socialists held that men should be allowed to possess only the property which was the result of their labour. There should not be any inequality by way of legal right of property by the state. If it so it should be destroyed forthwith to secure justice.

■■

IV

Giambattista Vico (1668–1744)

Giambattista Vico was the native of Naples. He was born on June 23, 1668 to a bookseller. Vico attended many schools in his early days. Although, he attended many schools, he was by and large self-educated. He took his law degree in 1694 from the University of Naples. For some time he served as Professor of rhetoric in the same University. In 1735, he was appointed to the high post of royal historiographer.

Vico, the Italian philosopher is renounced as the exponent of a "New science of humanity". He published his first work "On the Method of the studies of Our Time" in 1709. In the following year he published his another book "On the Ancient Wisdom of the Italians". His "Universal law" was published in 1720-22.

Vico has given a graphic picture about his theory of knowledge in his two books viz. "On the Method of the Studies of Our Time" and "On the Ancient Wisdom of the Italians". According to him, precise knowledge is possible in Mathematics through a process of abstraction and definition. The same method can be applied to the natural order to some extent. Hence, one can attain some knowledge. Since, the natural order is made by Nature or God, it is very difficult to measure the same as stated by Vico. The natural order can be completely known to God only because it was made by Him, whereas the human institutions, the civil world, social and political orders are made by men and so men can have knowledge about these. To vindicate and indicate his theory he says that there are three stages, three elements and three principles in everything. It is seen that men at first feel without observing fear of God, then they observe with terribly troubled mind, and finally, they reflect with a clear mind. These three represent the three stages of human history. These three stages give way for three corresponding forms of government i.e. theocracy, aristocracy and monarchy or republic.

In his "Universal Law" Vico points out clearly about rational civil theology of divine providence, principles of power and authority, evolution and growth of human ideas, natural law of nations and the principles of universal history. By employing his triad he says that history develops through a cycle of three stages i.e. divine, heroic and human. These three represent the three stages of human understanding. Finally, these three stages give way for three forms of government.

According to Vico, the historians will be able to bet the above eternal cycle, Men are historical beings subject to constant changes and evolution. Hence, history and understanding of political institutions must be based on the interpretation of historical date. So far as this point is concerned Vico gave a clear way for Hegel who later on gave his own ideas on the interpretation of history.

■■

V

Montesquieu (1689–1755)

Montesquieu, Charles Louis de Secondat de, was born on January 18, 1689 near Bordeaux. He was the son of a distinguished French lawyer. He studied law and in 1714 he was admitted to the grade of Counsellor. He greatly loved society and literature. In 1721, he published his "Persian Letters". It was a collection of letters which contained the existing social, political and religious institutions in France. He studied the histories of Rome, France, England, Egypt, Persia, Indo-China and Japan which left their deep impressions on the cultivated mind of the philosopher. He visited Austria, Hungary, Venice, Rome, Switzerland, the Rhine, Holland and England. After returning to his native place, he published his "Reflections on the causes of the Greatness and the Decadence of the Romans". His masterpiece "The Spirit of Laws" (Esprit des Lois) was published in 1748. He died in the year 1755.

Montesquieu has given a detailed account about the concept of law in his famous book "The Spirit of Laws". This concept of Law was borrowed by him from Aristotle. But there is a vast difference between the two. Aristotle applied it and limited it to the state level, whereas Montesquieu applied it to the whole universe.

From the time of Plato to the time of Locke different definitions have been given by different writers for the term "Law". On the contrary Montesquieu says, "Laws in the widest possible connotation are any necessary relations arising from a things, nature. In this sense all beings have their laws; the Deity His laws, the material world its laws, the intelligences superior to man their laws, man his laws ...". In other words, for Montesquieu any relation between one thing and some other thing is a law. The entire universe is regulated by laws. Man is a free agent but is subject to ignorance error and impetuous passions. Divine laws are hence very important in the world.

Divine laws are fixed and variable. Man has been reminded of his duty to God by these laws. Such a man is able to forget himself. The moral laws are there to lead him on the right path. He is liable to forget his fellow creatures and therefore legislators have made civil laws to remind his relations with other individuals. Prior to those Laws man was guided by the laws of Nature. The first law of Nature is peace and security. In the state of nature man would think of the preservation of his being. His foremost desire is to save himself from the surrounding dangers. He could hardly afford to be aggressive, unlike Hobbe's man in the state of nature. There is no question of conflict of war. After obtaining security that man would like to fulfil his wants, to seek food, clothing and shelter. Thus the second law deals about his nourishment. The natural law of association is considered as the third law. Finally man with his knowledge unites with his fellow beings and produces the natural law of a desire of living in society.

Natural Law serves as a base for the formation of society. In other words society is formed on the basis of natural law. According to Montesquieu, "As soon as man enters into a state of society he loses the sense of his weakness, equality ceases, and then commences the state of war." There begins a conflict in two directions between individuals and societies. This gives rise to positive law. There are three kinds of positive laws. They are the Civil Law, the Political or Constitutional Law, and International Law. The Civil Law regulates the relations of individual citizens. The Political or Constitutional Law seeks to regulate the relations between the governor and the governed. The International Law seeks to establish the relation between nation and nation. The law of nations is common to all, but positive and civil laws differ from society to society. The positive laws must be connected with the character of a people; and the civil laws must be related to topography, climate, size of population, religion of a people and so on. Moreover, these three laws must be related to one another. These views are seen in the Spirit of Laws. Here Montesquieu repudiates clearly social contract theory.

According to Montesquieu, state was the product of environment and organic and not conventional in nature. The laws of nature taught the man the desirability of peace and security, and of living in society in a friendly spirit.

Montesquieu was a political philosopher of his own time and was comparatively free from the influence of the institutions prevalent in those days in France. Hence, much ideas of sovereignty government rights of man, and natural rights are absent in his work.

In his "Spirit of Laws" Montesquieu analyses the different types of government and examines the characteristics of each different type. He asserted that there are three types of government viz. monarchy, republic and aristocracy. He further says, to Montesquieu, no form of government was essentially good in itself, its value was relative. If the spirit which characterised each form underwent change, a revolution in government necessarily followed. Democracy became impossible of political virtue and the spirit of equality disappeared. Aristocracy could not survive if moderation among the ruling classes ceased. Monarchy was impossible if honour grew weak among the rulers. Despotism by its native was unstable. Revolutions followed no regular sequence; the new form depended upon the conditions in each case.

Montesquieu says that certain religions had a definite affinity for certain forms of government. Protestantism goes well with a republican form of government Roman Catholicism with a monarchical form, while Mohammedanism and Despotism are well suited to each other. Further, he says that the size of the state also provides a basis for the classification of government. For e.g. republican form of government in small states monarchy in moderate states, despotism in big states etc.

Montesquieu followed Bodin in giving considerable attention to the influence of physical environment on the social economic, religious and political institutions of a country. Of these climate plays a prominent part. Climate influences character and institutions. Political liberty is natural in the colder climates; slavery in the warmer, mountainous regions are conducive to liberty the fertile plains to tyranny. The large geographical divisions of Asia favour despotism; the smaller units of Europe promote freedom.

Montesquieu was a fiery champion of liberty of the individual. He borrowed his ideas of liberty to some extent from John Locke. To him political liberty meant a relation between the state and the subjects. It meant the right of doing all that the laws permit. If a man or an individual violates law, he could not retain liberty because then everybody would violate law and there would be liberty from one. If the individual or a body of individuals are above the laws, there can be no liberty. In a despotism, liberty is not secure because of the reasoned caprice of an individual ruler. Regarding civil right he has not given any precise definition. According to him liberty can exist only where the possessors of governmental powers are subject to limitations. Political liberty can exist only where separation of powers and system of checks and balances is enshrined in the constitutional system.

Montesquieu found in the separation of the three powers of government-executive legislative and judicial the best guarantee for liberty. He was of the opinion that if the legislative power is in the hands of one person or of one body of official, there can be no liberty nor can there be any liberty if the power to judge is not separated from the legislative and executive powers. According to his theory different persons or different body of persons should administer the three organs of government. No one should control the other. Under this situation the liberty of the individual could be preserved. If those powers are concentrated in the hands of a single person or in the hands of group of persons, the liberty of the citizen will be in danger. From this it is very clear that the liberty of the citizen should be ensured by the separation of powers.

The view of Montesquieu was that the stability of the English constitution was due to the fact there was a separation of powers in that country. He arrived this conclusion after paying a visit to England. The practical application of the theory is to be found in the constitution of U.S.A. The constitution provided for an independent President, an independent Congress and an independent Supreme Court and the election of the judges in the states and the governors in the states. Thinking that absolute separation of powers would lead to stalemate, the framers of the constitution therefore adopted the system of checks and balances.

Liberty was writ large on the "Espritdes Lois" but there was no democrat according to R.C. Gupta. He did not believe in popular sovereignty. He was a sort of French whig and his whiggism considerably influences political theory in the 19th Century.

Criticisms : The Theory of Separation of Powers has been severely and seriously criticised by many scholars. Firstly, it cannot be accepted literally. It is true only in part. It is very difficult to divide the departments of the governments into three well defined water tight compartments one having nothing to do with the other. Secondly, a rigid separation must lead to inarticulation and deadlocks. In this connection Laski says, "in practice moreover it is impossible to maintain any rigorous separation ....." Thirdly, Montesquieu insisted on the intimate relation between liberty and separation of powers. However, experience shows that there exists no such relation between the two. Even in the case of American Constitution no separation of powers could save the liberty of the American people. Fourthly, the growth of administrative law is opposed to the theory of separation of powers. Fifthly, the separation of powers results in jealousy, suspicion and internal friction. Finally, the growth of the powers of political parties is making the separation of powers meaning less. The party in power controls both the legislature and the executive.

The chief function of the government according to Montesquieu was therefore maintenance of political liberty and creation of such climate as would ensure civil liberty amongst the people. His writings reveal that he had on his mind a deep imprint of what Aristotle wrote and thought of political institutions. Hence, some political thinkers to the extent saying that Montesquieu was Aristotle of 19th Century.

■ ■

VI
Voltaire (1694–1778)

Voltaire was one of the greatest philosophers of the world. He was a French man. He was born on Nov. 21, 1694. He lost his mother when he was very young. He had no affection towards his father. He was very fond of literature. The religious instructions of the Jesuit Fathers served only to excite his skcpticism and mockery. The French military disasters of 1709 and the horrors of religious persecutions distressed him very much. Twice he was confined in the Bastille prison for his verbal battles with the government and the church. As a result he decided to uphold the rights of men of letters against the arbitrary power of the king and of the nobles.

Voltaire went over to England in 1726 and spent three years there along with English scholars. Further he admired the English liberal outlook and the Freedom in the discussion of religious and philosophic questions. Returning to France, he decided to show England as a model for his countrymen.

"History of Charles XII" and "Philosophical Letters" were published by him in 1731 and 1734 respectively. In the above letters he has given his criticisms of Descartes and Pascal, Voltaire says that the purpose of life is not to reach heaven through penitence but to assure happiness to all men by progress in both the sciences and arts a fulfilment for which their nature is destined. Moreover the above letters embody the philosophy of the 18th Century and is a landmark in the history of political thought.

As a result of the publication of these letters he had to run away from the inevitable arrest warrant. He was given refuge by Mme. du. Chatelet. Then fame and friendship earned by him in

Belgium, Cirey and Paris paved for his success in life. Once again doom and disaster embraced him after the death of Chatelet, So he took refuge at Geneva.

"The Age of Louis XIV" and "History of Mankind" the two great works are still considered as great contributions to cultural history. After 1758 he was aptly called as the inkeeper of Europe since he lived a crowded life with worldwide fame.

Voltaire's main target of attack was the Roman Catholic Church. He constructed a personal encyclopaedia in 1764 which was later enlarged. He was able to retain the leadership of the philosophic movement by speaking and acting against the injustice done to the people by an intolerant church. He was given a warm welcome when he returned to Paris in 1778 where he died towards the end of May.

Voltaire condemned organised Christianity for its basic belief in the supernatural and for what he held to be its support of social injustice. Hence he was of the opinion that the middle ages was a period of barbarous misery. He hated the jews for their begotten Christianity. In his "Treatise on Toleration" he writes that a fanaticism composed of superstition and ignorance has been the sickness of all the centuries.

In his "Philosophical Dictionary" which was published in 1764 he gives clear picture about his anti clerical thoughts and his doubts about the historicity of biblical characters. He further says that the church and the state should be separated from one another with a view to make the state free and secular. He shuns metaphysics and holds theology in contempt.

Another interesting aspect of Volatire's thought it is the place he attributed to reason in human nature, "That which our eyes and mathematics demonstrate to us, we must hold to be true. In all the rest we must say only, I do not know."

Voltaire wa$ not a defender of enlightened despotism nor was he a democrat. He had firm belief in historical cycles. He had good hopes of four cultural events like Periclean Athens, Augustian Rome, Renaissance Italy and France under Louis XIV. But he had great devotion to Enlightenment. His famous saying that "If God did not exist, it would be necessary to invent Him", has often been misinterpreted as to stamp him as an atheist. He not only attacked atheism but also orthodoxy in his works.

Voltaire was a radical in religious matters but he was a conservative in the matters of politics. Theoretically, he stands for republic. He considers that men are rarely worthy to govern themselves. According to him, monarchy was the most permanent and fittest form of government. That monarchy would be in absolute power. He was for drastic administrative and legal reforms. He was against arbitrary arrest, secret trials of privileges etc. He demanded equitable justice and a new penal code so that torture and death sentence would be abolished.

Voltaire regarded patriotism and nationalism as sentimental fallacy. On this basis he condemned the American colonies who rebelled against established government. On the other hand, he cherished and nourished the ideal of world citizenship. He further stood for centralisation of powers on the basis of freedom. He condemned Rousseau's call to go back to nature. His writings along with the Rousseau greatly influenced the French people during the French Revolution. Voltaire had better and larger vision than Rousseau. However, Voltaire occupies a great place in the history of Political Thought.

■ ■

VII

David Hume (1711–1776)

David Hume was a great Scottish Philosopher; he was also a great historian, economist and essayist. During his early days, he was very interested in literature and philosophy. After his 15th year he began to study Law. But in 1729 he was seriously affected by a nervous breakdown. It took him a few years to recover from that breakdown.

'A Treatise of Human Nature', 'Political Discourses' : 'A History of England' (Four Volumes) and 'Moral and Political Essays' were published by Hume. For some time he held the post of Secretary to the British Ambassador in Paris and Under Secretary of State *i.e.* from 1763 to 1769. For the rest of his life, he lived as a philosopher and a historian. His Dialogues concerning 'Natural Religion' was published posthumously in 1779. He died on 25th August, 1776 at the age of 65.

Hume's Political ideas : According to Hume's ethical theory that an action as vicious is to state a fact about it or, in other words, that moral judgements are true or false in the same sense that "Judgements of reason" are true or false. He reiterates that the viciousness of an act resides in its effect upon our feelings as human beings. The actions that are in the interest of humanity arouse our moral feelings.

As regards political theory, Hume rejects the conception of natural law, natural rights and social contract. He criticises the political parties in his essays on political theory. According to him the influence of the parties is destructive. As soon as a political party is formed the men in the party develop or contract an affection to the person with whom they are united and an animosity against their antagonists. They transmit these passions to posterity. At the same time Hume came to the conclusion that party system is an unavoidable one.

Hume says that political society was not established for the administration of justice. It did not come into existence at one time. It appeared at the time of war. During the war the superior man asserted his power over others. As a result the people bowed before that superior man. Hume believed that force brought the state into existence the state was sustained by the principal of utility and public opinion. Hence, force is very essential to receive the obedience of the people. Like force, public opinion is also very essential for the governments to enforce obedience in the state.

Hume's political philosophy is based partly on Lockean ideas. He opposed the rationalistic school and their philosophy based on their conception of the law of nature. He condemned and criticised both the theories of Divine Right and Social contract as the basis of the origin of the state. He said that both were lacking in factual foundation; both were absurd in practical purposes; both were speculative in character.

On the historical point of view Hume attacked the social contract theory since it could not have taken place among the primitive people due to lack of reasoning and intelligence. Further we cannot give any example from history according to Hume.

Hume was an anti-religionist during his life time. He hated religion. He was of the opinion that religion made people bad both individually and collectively. It was a great stumbling block for the progress of society. He considered the church a department of the state.

Hume stood for a perfect commonwealth. He was a conservative by temperament. He was in support of absolute government. He did not like popular government. He considered it a mob-rule. Monarchical type of government was preferred by him because it has some advantages over the republican in regard to liberty. Added to this it is more stable and steady; it is more continuous and constant, it is more congenial and conducive to steady advancement of true liberty. Hume agrees with James

Harrington that landed property determines the nature of government. In other words economic factor determines the form of government. At the same time he does not make property as the foundation of all political forces.

According to Hume liberty is the perfection of civil society. He emphasises the importance of government. It is also very necessary to the people, because it is a useful institution. This factor is the basis of obedience. The chief duty of the government is to protect the people and their property. Another duty of the government is the enforcement of contracts.

Hume condemns revolution. He says that more evil will result from it than good. Hence he dislikes the changes through revolution and violent methods.

Hume says that man should not accumulate wealth. It is always dangerous to society if his main object is to accumulate wealth. He further adds that every person has the right to enjoy the fruits of his labour. But he believed that utility was the foundation of the state.

It is seen from the above views that David Hume was an appraiser more than a formulator of political ideas.

■■

VIII

Jean Jacques Rousseau (1712–1778)

Coker in his ''Readings in Political Philosophy'' has given a beautiful account about the early life and works of Rousseau in a lucid manner. Rousseau was born of a poor family in Geneva on June 28, 1712. His ancestors came and settled in Geneva from France in the middle of the 16th century as religious refugees. He lost his mother when he was very young. Later on he used to say, ''I cost my mother her life and my birth was the first of my misfortunes.'' Since his father was a watchmaker and a dancer he was not able to give proper education to his son. He had no stable or practical training of any sort. He ran away from home when sixteen years of age and thereafter for twenty years he led a wandering life. He saw much of Europe ''through the eyes of a penniless and at times hunted, vagabond, who did not always know where his next meal come from and where he would sleep.'' During these days of great stresses and strain he took some note of the ideas and feelings of the poorer people with whom he came into contact; and in his sojourns he devoted some attention to the study of philosophy. While he was in Paris he came into contact with the Encyclopaedists. Hence he established himself at Paris and did some miscellaneous writing. Diderot accepted him as contributor to the Encyclopaedia. For ''His character, his outlook on life, his scale of values, his instinctive reactive reactions, all differed essentially from what the Enlightenment regarded as admirable.'' Thus Sabine describes his condition. It was difficult for him, therefore to establish lasting human relations, except with Lesvaeuran uneducated woman, with whom he lived for about twenty years.

Rousseau gained a general literary reputation in 1749. In the same year the Academy of Dijon announced a prize for his essay entitled' "Has the progress of sciences and arts contributed to corrupt or purify morals." He published the essay in 1751 under the title "A Discourse on the Moral Effects of the Arts and Sciences." According to Rousseau, "Our minds have been corrupted in proportion as the arts and sciences have improved. He further charged that we have physicists, geometricians, chemists, astronomets, poets, musicians and painters in plenty, but we have no longer a citizen among us."

Rousseau published his "Discourse on the origin of Inequality" in 1755. In this work he distinguishes between natural and moral or political equality in a clear cut manner. His 'Discourse on political Economy' was published in Diderots Encyclopaedia in 1755. The 'Social Contract' the Bible of the French Revolution was published in 1762. Of all his works, the Social Contract is regarded as the most famous work in the history of political thought. It is in the Social Contract that Rousseau's idea of the state is most clearly seen. In 1762, he also published his "Emile" a revolutionary treatise on education. This aroused vigorous opposition from political and ecclesiastical leaders due to its dogmas of revealed religion. Since, there was danger of prosecution he ran away to Switzerland. There he was welcomed for his ideas. In England, too he met the same warm welcome. He was able to return to France in 1767 and spent the last decade of his life in retirement completing his confessions . He died in 1778.

Estimate: According to Bergson, His (Rousseau's) was the most powerful of the influences which the human mind has experienced since Descartes. His influence greatly affected the mind of the world on par with other men. C.L. Wayper says that he left the stamp of his strong and original genius on politics, education, religion, literature, and it is hardly an exaggeration to say with Langson that he is to be found at the entrance to all the paths leading to the present. Yet, there has been no writer about whom it has been more difficult in to find agreement than about Rousseau. He has been greatly landed and more maligned at the same time.

Rousseau is considered as the extreme individualist, the latest and greatest of the individualist political theorists. He is also regarded as the greatest absolutist and at the same time the precursor of the 19th century German idealism. Constant said of him, "He is the most terrible ally of despotism in all its forms." Duguit wrote, "J-J. Rousseau is the father of Jacobin despotism, of Caesarian dictatorship and the inspirer of the absolutist doctrines of Kant and of Hegel." To put it in a nutshell he is both extreme individualist and extreme absolutist.

Rousseau revived the classical Aristotlean view that man is a political animal whose nature can be filled only in the state. Plato's emphasis that the state is a matter of ethics rather than of law is also reflected in Rousseau's thought. Both Aristotle and Plato stood for good government at the expense of self-government. Locke and the liberals pleaded for self-government relegating the problem of good government into the background. Rousseau tried to synthesize both. Hence, he is welcomed by the adherents of both organic theory of state and the liberals.

The Social Contract theory is the most ancient theory. It is the most important of all the theories regarding the origin of the state. It has played a prominent role in modern political theory and practice.

Jean Jacques Rousseau the great French philosopher gave his ideas about this theory elaborately and excellently in the "Social Contract" and "Emile". The Social Contract the Bible of the French Revolution was published in 1762. The main substance of this theory is that the state is the result of an agreement entered into by men who originally had no government organisation.

Rousseau's ideas on the state are clearly found in his "Social Contract". This work opens with the remark "man is born free and everywhere he is in chains. One who believes himself the master of the rest is only more of a slave than they. How does that change about? I do not know what can render it legitimate? That question I think I can answer." Thus, Rousseau seeks to answer the question, "What is the state and why should I obey it?" Hence, he says that authority of man over man can have no rational basis except through agreement and consent.

The corner stone of Rousseau's Social Contract theory was the state of nature. According to him, Man by nature never thinks and he who thinks is a corrupt creature. During the state of nature the people enjoyed unlimited freedom. They had no private property of their own. They did not know about competition, hatred and jealousy. They did not know whether a particular thing was good or bad, right or wrong and useful or useless. Thus, the people of Rousseau enjoyed innocent life of perfect freedom and equality in the state of nature.

Many years passed on and a drastic change took place in their attitude. It was due to two reasons. One was the increase in population and the other was the dawn of reason. By the process of increasing population many progressive changes took place in the field of economics. As a result the people who lived in the state of nature lost their happiness, freedom and simplicity. Every men in the society became selfish; there was rivalry; there was enmity; there was suspicion and hatred. They quarrelled themselves. So there were wars and murders everywhere. They wanted to save their life and property from danger. Hence, they sought for the formation of a civil society. This led to a social contract.

Accordingly every individual gave up his rights to the community. The community became all powerful with enormous powers. It became sovereign. The sovereignty of the community is inalienable and indivisible. In this contract the people voluntarily made the contract.

The social contract is not a contract which men made with their future ruler. Government is only their agent. If men are placed under the rule of some individuals or community it would mean slavery. But men have come together to fulfil nature which makes slavery impossible. Hence, they must create a society "in such a way that each when united to his fellows renders obedience to his own will and remains as free as he was before." It should be noted here that the 'sovereign' means in Rousseau not the monarch or the government but the community in its collective and legislative capacity.

Rousseau says that law alone is responsible for the obedience of men. It is to law that men owe justice and liberty. Here the question arises what is the law? Rousseau calls it the universal voice. It is the voice of the General will.

General will : The conception of the "general will" plays a very important part in Rousseau's system. What is the General will? It is the will of all the citizens when they are willing not their own private interests but the general good. According to Rousseau, the will of the sovereign which is always right is the "general will." Every individual is allowed to will his own will and the majority will is formed. The general will is for the general welfare. The social contract involves that whoever refuses to obey the general will shall be forced to do so. This means nothing less than that he will be forced to be free. This idea of being forced to be free is very metaphysical in nature.

Rousseau says that the General will is not identical with the will of the majority. He distinguishes between our will for our selfish ends and our will for the general good. For common interest everybody is allowed to convey his will and thus the majority will is found, when we demand something not for us but for everyone, our will is general.

The general will deals with matters of public interest. At the same time it deals with private interest also. Although, other societies and associations may have a General will in relation to their members, a relation to the state their will is particular. The General will of the state is the most comprehensive of all.

According to Rousseau, the General will is inalienable and indivisible. Hence, it cannot be represented in parliamentary institutions. "As soon as a nation appoints representatives" he says it is no longer free, it no longer exists. He declared that "England was only free during elections, after which it is unsaved and counts for nothing." The General will cannot therefore be represented, because representative assemblies tend to develop particular interests of their own. It cannot be delegated in any way. He stated "the moment there is a master, there is no longer a sovereign." As such, nothing less than all the people together can be trusted to will the general will ... As Rousseau expressed it, it is only "the voice of the people is the voice of God."

The General will must be a will which is general in every sense and which is particular in none. According to the agreement of the contract the General will must respect the wishes of every citizen since they come under integral part of our group.

The General will of Rousseau cannot be an executive will. The people ought not to be responsible for the details of government. Here he clearly distinguishes the difference between the Government and the sovereign people. The people entrusts its executive power to its agent whereas the government retain some limited right of supervision over it. So long as the General will is sovereign it does not matter if the government is a democracy, an aristocracy, or a monarchy — whichever in the existing circumstances is most suitable will be the best. However, Rousseau prefers democracy since it is too prefect for men. He considers that men are too imperfect for kingship since kings have of becoming tyrants. Similarly, he condemns hereditary aristocracy as the worst type of all forms of government.

According to Rousseau, the General will is infallible. He says that it is always right and tends to the public advantage i.e. men must never forget that they come together for the sake of good life and should do nothing to make that good life impossible.

In spite of his above views on the General will he finds some vagueness in the will perhaps it reflects his belief that it would never be easy for men to will it. The illustration of General will that he gives in Emile is a sufficient proof for the same.

Criticisms : The theory of social contract has been criticised on many grounds. 1. On the basis of history the theory has been considered as mere fiction. We can not give even a single example for history to show that the state has been created as a result of voluntary agreement.

2. Sir Henry Maine has criticised the social contract theory on the ground that it is based on wrong assumptions. He further says that contract is not the beginning but the end of society. In primitive society the people had not such freedom to enter into a contract.

3. Since the contract is made by the individuals it can remain

as long as there is sweet will and co-operation among them. Otherwise there can be no end to it.

4. Bluntschli and others point out that theory is dangerous. For e.g. Rousseau had intimate connection with French Revolution. The advocates of this theory actually encourage revolution.

5. The conception of natural rights and natural liberty as is said to have existed in the state of nature is illogical and fallacious.

6. According to this theory men were equals in the state of nature. This view is not correct because Von Haller the German jurist says that inequality rather than equality is natural.

7. Critics have pointed out that Rousseau's "General will" is abstract one; it is very narrow. It is also mentioned that the General will is neither general nor will. Usually it can be decided by the majority decision. It will definitely pave a way for the state absolutism. According to T.H. Green will not force is the basis of the state, is clearly seen in democracies.

The social contract became the Bible of most of the leaders in the French Revolution, but no doubt as the fate of Bible, it was not carefully read and was still understood by many of its disciples. However it cannot be denied that the states began to have written constitutions after Locke and Rousseau.

Comparison — Rousseau Hobbes and Locke

The approach of Hobbes, Locke and Rousseau in respect of Social Contract theory is different from person to person. The approaches to society, government, rights, liberty, property and the place of man in the society made by the three writers showed considerable variations. Hobbes and Rousseau held that the state is the result of a contract entered into by men who originally lived in the state of nature. There was only one contract and in that contract the individuals surrendered all their rights to the sovereign. The sovereign was absolute in character. But Rousseau did not agree with Hobbes that the government was absolute. He made the government dependent upon the people and thereby accepted the conclusions of Locke. According to Rousseau the individual surrendered his rights not to the ruler but to the community.

Further he made a very clear distinction between the state and the government. In the above points Rousseau was in conformity with Locke rather than Hobbes.

Rousseau advocated the complete surrender of rights to the sovereign; Locke stood for a limited sovereignty; Rousseau stood for popular sovereignty; Hobbes stood for absolute sovereignty. The state of nature of Hobbes was both pre-social and pre-political whereas Locke's was only pre-political.

Rousseau's man in the state of nature was a noble savage. He was primitive by nature. He was independent; self-sufficient, contented, healthy and fearless instinct played a very good role in regulating his life.

Hobbes was for a doctrinaire, sordid, rigid and absolute society. Rousseau was all for a free, unfettered, unchained and unregulated man. He also preferred a type of vagabond life since he himself led the life of a vagabond in his early days. The approach of Rousseau is a balanced approach between these two extremes.

In the case of Rousseau there is only one contract; but in the case of Locke there are two contracts. The social contract gave a decent burial to the state of Nature and substituted for it a civil society or the state. The contract between the government and the ruler was formed by the government. In the second contract, the government was a party to the contract.

Since, Hobbes stood for absolutism he could be said to be nearer Fascist, Nazist and the totalitarian regimes. Rousseau could be said to be nearer anarchist and the communist conception of things but for the fact that he was a strong protagonist of freedom and lesser and lesser authority of the state on men, the communist state is the opposite of it. Locke can be considered to be a forerunner of all parliamentary and democratic governments.

According to Hobbes, the natural man was selfish in character; he was envious, dejected and quarrelsome. The state of nature was a gloomy state. It was a state of constant welfare. According to Rousseau, the natural man was good; he was pleasant and happy. The state of nature was a state of bliss and happiness. According to Locke, the state of nature was neither too good nor one of constant warfare. It was not convenient and comfortable due to the absence of an authority to enforce the rights of man in the state of nature.

Hobbes remarked that if there was a change in government there would be dissolution in the state; the people would return to the state of nature. Locke had a firm belief that the people had the supreme right to have their own government. They could bring a change in the government if they found it unsatisfactory. To Rousseau the government was merely the agent or the tool to execute the popular will.

From the Social Contract theory of Hobbes we know that law was the command of the sovereign. To Locke law must be the expression of the will of the people and it should be consistent with the law of reason. According to Rousseau law is merely the expression of the general will.

Locke's people in the social contract had the right of revolution. Hobbes too gave his people the right to transfer their allegiance when the sovereign was not able to protect their lives. In the case of Rousseau there was no such right for revolt to his people.

Whatever may be the merits of the practicability of Rousseau's writings, political philosophers who came after him found his writings very useful. The Declaration of Independence in America the Bill of Rights, the Revolution of 1688 (Glorious Revolution) and the American War of Independence all owe their origins to the writings of Rousseau.

IX
Immanuel Kant (1724–1804)

Immanuel Kant, the father of idealist philosophy and the great German philosopher was born at Korigsberg on 22nd April, 1724. His father was a poor saddler; his mother was an uneducated but intelligent Pietiest. After completing his education, he had to spend 9 years as private tutor to qualify himself from the university. In 1770 he was appointed as Professor of Logic and Metaphysics in the same University. He had a very low opinion of women and did not marry. He died as a confirmed bachelor on 12th February, 1804.

Kant's ideas of philosophy are mostly taken from Rousseau and Montesquieu. He borrowed his ideas from others and fitted them into his own philosophy. The period from 1770 to 1790 formed a brightest period in his philosophical works. In his three chief works viz. "Critique of Pure Reason", "Critique of Practical Reason" and "Critique of Judgement", we find his more ideas about morality than of politics. Further his political ideas are to be found in his works like "Metaphysical First principles of the Theory of Law." "Perpetual Peace", "The Principles of Political Right" and "The Natural Principle of the Political Order."

(i) *Respect for Personality* : Kant's philosophy was essentially individualistic in character. He gave the highest place for the free will of the individual in his political thought. According to him, every individual was an end in himself and no one was to be considered as a means to an end. Further he had a soft corner for the liberty of the individuals and he was not ready to sacrifice the same for the sake of the state.

(ii) *Rights and Duties*: According to Kant, the rights and

duties of individuals should be respected. At the same time he said "Liberty consists in the power to do anything which inflicts no injury on one's neighbour." One man's rights should not injure other man's freedom. A right is also a burden and an obligation. According to Kant, duty was self-imposed. Hence, Vaughan remarks, "Right expands into freedom and freedom expands into right."

(iii) *The Social Contract* : Though, Kant accepted the idea of social contract he did not find any connection of the same with the origin of the state such a thing was irrelevant and dangerous. He further said that man could be compelled to obey a law which he did not accept of his own accord. Thus, his social contract is a constitutional compact by means of which a form of government is established and that compact binds the government and the people. The same contract does not bring about a change from a state of nature to an organised state.

(iv) *Moral philosophy* : In his "Critique of pure Reason" he gives a clear critical analysis of pure reason. According to him, a reason independent of all sense experience is called pure reason. It is knowledge belonging to the structure of mind. It is superior to knowledge. The absolute truths about the existence could be known only by pure reason. It can be practical i.e. it can itself determine the will independently of any thing empirical. He tries to find a universal and necessary ethic; a prior principles of morals which are absolute and certain. According to him, moral sense is innate, and not derived from experience. Man is truly free who is also morally free. He has coined the phrase autonomy of the moral will. Acts are moral only if they are done on principles which should conform certain norms. These norms are known as categorical imperatives. By this one can determine whether a particular act is good or not, moral or not.

There are three imperatives according to Kant (1) "Act as if the maxim of our action were to become by our will a universal law of nature." (2) "Act as to treat humanity whether in thine own person or in that of another in every case as an end, never only as a means." (3) "Act as if you were through your maxims a law making member of a kingdom of ends." Firstly, we are supposed to avoid behaviour, if adopted by all men would render social life impossible. Secondly, every individual can achieve perfection in himself and happiness in others. Thirdly, all laws should be outcome of agreement among rational beings and not the effect of a mythical law given. Finally, he says that man is free as long as his will is free and his will is free when it is acting according to the categorical imperatives.

(v) *Property* : The institution of private property has accepted by Kant. But he was not in favour of the individualistic view regarding private property. For the expression of will of man the institution of private property was very essential. According to Kant the possession of property was a derived, right. It was not the gift of nature to man.

(vi) *Punishments* : Punishments should not be inflicted upon the criminals for the sake of vengeance. They should not be tortured or terrorised by way of punishments. Punishments did not involve any idea of reformation of the individual.

(vii) *Concept of Law*: According to Kant that law can neither be the command of the sovereign nor be based on custom or tradition or precedent. Generally a sovereign could not act against pure reason. The laws which are formulated contrary to the pure reason and the laws which are not in conformity with priori principles are immoral and hence null and void. The trespassers of law should be visited by punishment.

(viii) *Civil state*: Kant's philosophy was based on individualism. He could not give too much power to the state. Man is egoistic by nature. Their love for power gain and glory and the effect of those glories is the war of all against all." Moral freedom should be promoted by individuals themselves and not by the state. It is the primary duty of the state to remove all barriers to liberty.

In his treatment of state and government there were three and two forms respectively. The three forms of state were autocracy, aristocracy and democracy. Republican and despotic were the two forms of government. As stated by Kant there are three powers in every state. They are the legislative executive and the judicial.

The first two powers must be separated for the sake of liberty. The two forms of government were republican and despotic "according as there is or is not a separation of the legislative and the executive power." According to Kant the form of government which was not representative was not rational and the function of the representative may be performed by the king or the nobility or the elected deputies From this view of Kant we know that he favoured constitutional monarchy and opposed despotism.

Kant was extremely opposed to any kind of violence. That could be expected of him because he was a philosopher. In his opinion the citizen had no right of revolution. He stood for legal change in constitutional set up of the state.

Creation of the World State

The Law of development or the Law of evolution is one of the most important philosophical thinkings of Kant. His development of law takes its growth from a lower to a higher level. It was concerned with the developments inside the human species and pre-supposed the survival of the best. He attempted to give the historical development of social and political institutions with his law of progress in the past and then predict their further developments.

According to Kant there was no reason or moral sense in the primitive society. They were dominated by instincts of self-preservation sexual desires, a desire for glory and ego for dominating other people. At the same time there was social intercourse; there was friendly co-operation and there was desire for company. Kant calls this as the un-social sociability of mankind. This paved the way for a warfare in the primitive society. Conflict and competition prevailed in the primitive society. It was due to the two kinds of instincts viz., to associate as well as to dominate. Both good and bad results were the outcome of that warfare. It forced the primitive men to develop his reasoning powers latent in him. The state of nature was so horrible. He willingly sacrificed his own lawless liberty and voluntarily submitted himself to the political state in which all men are subject to uniform laws. Hence the creation of the political state is considered as a landmark in the history of human progress.

Man developed from the savage condition i.e. from the beastly condition to that of a life dominated by reason and moral law. According to Kant this is not the apex in the evolution of human progress. The mutual antagonism of man brought into existence the creation of state. The mutual hatred of states will bring about a federation comprising of all states in the world, capable of creating eternal and everlasting peace. There is no safety for each state in the world. One is afraid of the other. The will to subjugate or encroach upon others is always there and preparations of defence which often render peace even more burdensome and destructive of internal warfare than war itself can never slacken. For this purpose international justice is to be founded upon public laws. Every state must submit before this law.

In his Essay on Perpetual Peace, he gave some purposeful suggestions for world peace. But his idea of Balance of Power was somewhat confusing. He denounced both secret diplomacy and secret societies since they would deceive the people and the governments. The first and the best guarantee of perpetual peace is the well integrated constitutional state such as is found in a republic.

Usually the actions of the government rest upon the will of the people in a republican state. War can be waged with its consent. So also peace can be made with its willingness. If they did not require any more war they can put an end to it. Because no nation will be willing to take upon itself the sufferings of a war. In this connection Kant pre-supposed popular sovereignty in the federation of all states. If such was not the case, the right of a nation to make its own decisions of place or war might place it in a dangerous situation. So Kant said that there should be world republic. World peace thus depends upon the relations of the citizens of the world states.

According to Kant international law should be maintained in preventing war and preserving peace. He intended that the civil constitution of every state should be republican and war shall not be declared except by a plebiscite of all the citizens. It has prospects of bringing about perpetual peace.

The ultimate goal of Kant was a free association of free peoples. In his "Jurisprudence" published in 1797, Kant put forth the suggestion of a permanent Congress of states. It should be given arbitrary powers. The same idea was realised to some extent by the united nations.

Many criticisms have been levelled against the philosophy of Kant by many writers. Firstly his philosophy too abstract to be understood by the ordinary people. Secondly Kant could not make up his mind as to whether he stood for freedom both in the ordinary sense and in the higher sense. Thirdly Vaughan says that Kant failed because "he hovered between the two entirely different conceptions of the state. He tossed between individualism and idealisms". Fourthly according to critics his philosophy is without content. His theories and doctrines are too abstract and make empirical approach impossible.

It cannot be denied that "Kant ushered in a new epoch in philosophical thought. His major writings constitute a milestone in the history of philosophy, he is one of these great and profound thinkers who by their works, but also by their lives, exercised a lasting influence upon the intellectual life of their own time and posterity...." F. Hebbel called him a thinker who moved and shook the world much more forcibly than his contemporary Frederick the Great, with all his Canon." Of all the contributions his ethical theory based on categories imperatives is a major contribution to the democratic ideal. By this contribution he has earned a very good name and fame in the history of political thought. In short his conception of state and individual is undoubtedly a great contribution in the political field.

■■

X

Edmund Burke (1729–1797)

Introduction : Edmund Burke is one of the most important political philosophers of the world. He is one of the most well known leading figures in English history. He was a sincere statesman; excellent orator; pre-eminent political thinker. He is rated as one of the world's greatest orators. John Bowk says that "Like Rousseau he was a phrase maker of the first order and more than Rousseau a lord of language in the finest lineage of political thought. Yet by origin and temperament, Burke was profoundly un-English."

Early life : Edmund Burke was born in the year 1729. His father was a protestant solicitor; his mother was a catholic lady. They gave him excellent education. He took his education in the Trinity College, Dublin. After completing his education there, he went to London to study Law. Since he had no interest in studying law he discontinued the same. For some time he was in England and France.

His Works : Edmund Burke published many works. They are (i) "A Vindication of Natural Society" (ii) "A Philosophical Enquiry into the Origin of our Ideas of the Sublime and Beautiful" (iii) "The Annual Register" (iv) "Thought on the causes of the Present discontents" (v) "Reflections on the Revolution in France" (vi) "Appeal from the New to the Old Whigs" (vii) "Letters on a Regicide Peace". Regarding America his best known statements were two parliamentary speeches, "On American Taxation" and "On Moving this Resolutions for conciliation with America." Regarding India his best known speeches were "On Mr. Fox's East Indian Bill" and "On the Nabob of Arcot's Debts."

Edmund Burke married Jane Nugent in 1757. She was the daughter of an Irish Catholic doctor. His political philosophy is not completely available in his single work as that of the "Spirit of Laws" of Montesquieu, "Leviathan" of Hobbes and "The Prince of Machiavelli". But his philosophy is available from his various contributions in a scattered form. Burke died at Beaconsfield, Buckinghamshire on 9th July, 1797.

His Views : Burke's ideas of society and state were in direct antithesis to John Locke. It is stated already that Locke's state was a product of social contract. According to Burke it was not so i.e. it was not created by any social contract. To Burke civil society was made by man himself; it was a product of man's practical intellect working after a basic pattern established by nature. Man perfects his nature through civil society. By nature he is rational and so the civil society is his natural state. Burke's view is that the state has been created to perfect his work to achieve good and moderate life and to promote the welfare. To the people the state is considered as the means which is ordained by nature. For that purpose the state should be given sovereign power. The people must acknowledge the same. According to Burke the people are not the masters of the state. In short there is no distinction and difference between state and society.

According to Locke the people enjoyed certain rights prior to the existence of the state. He termed those rights as natural rights. To Burke the rights exist only in the state and not outside the state. If there is no state there can be no rights. In addition to this he claims that civil rights should be extended to all whereas the political rights should be given only to those who are having the capacity to enjoy and ability to exercise those rights.

Burke gave a new theoretical synthesis to suit the political atmosphere of those days of Whig and Tory. The new theoretical synthesis was of Whig principal of freedom and the Tory principle of order. They were the following (1) religious establishment should respect the conscience of the dissenter, (2) aristocracy should leave some limited room for the upward mobility of new talent, (3) tradition must be adjusted, and (4) an imperial nation can maintain order only by respecting the traditions of its colonies.

The key to national prosperity is individual freedom in the economic field according to Burke. His colonial policy is considered a noteworthy feature of his political philosophy. During the American war of Independence he gave whole hearted support for the colonies in the parliament. One of the most important drastic steps taken by the mother country was the introduction of Stamp Act. It was not only damnable but also dangerous one. In 1776 he spoke for the repeal of the Stamp Act as concession to American feelings. At the same time he did not hesitate to support the Declaratory Act which gave the constitutional right to his country to tax the colonists. In this connection it is the duty of the students of political thought to mention about his two famous speeches in Parliament. They are best known in the world. They are (i) "On American Taxation" (1774) and (ii) Moving his Resolutions for conciliation with America" (1775).

Burke's interest in India also cannot be minimised. He in the 1760s and 1770s opposed the interference of English Government in the affairs of the company as a violation of charter rights.

Burke is rightly considered to be the founder and defender of modern conservation. He put more stress on tradition. His conservatism was due to his implicit faith in Divine will. He was a great religious man. He was not a democrat. He favoured aristocracy.

Burke's greatest work "Reflections on the Revolutions in France" was published after his first speech against the revolution in 1790. He condemned it as a catastrophe. It was for the leaders only. The motive of the revolution was not so meaningful. He favoured the real rights of man. He wanted that these rights of man to be made moderate and practical by way of "prescription".

Burke was not a die-hard. He favoured liberalism also. He hated uniformity and opposed equality. Further he opposed universal adult franchise. Political thinkers like Stephen, Thomas Morely and H.J. Laski described Burke as a utilitarian. Burke received inspiration from David Hume. According to Laski the metaphysics of Burke are largely those of David Hume.

His conservative ideas : Edmund Burke is one of the most

well known figures in English history. He was a sincere statesman; he was a prominent political thinker; he was a great parliamentary orator. He played an important role in all major political issues for about 30 years after 1765. Hence he remains as an important figure in the history of political thought.

Burke's conservative ideas are found in his works. He is considered to be the founder and defender of modern conservatism. He realised that the basis of conservation is not force but tradition, that it can be defended not by repression of the opponent but by the gentle force of persuasion and education. That is why he was called the exponent of conservation. Sabine writes that, "Burke is rightly regarded as the founder of self conscious political conservatism."

Though Burke was the defender of modern conservatism, he never failed to realise that the basis of conservatism is not force but tradition. Hence he laid emphasis on tradition. He had great regard and respect for all old things. "Old is gold" the old saying was keenly observed by him. He thought that these things are valuable because they had existed for a long time and had attained maturity. Added to this he had great respect for the wisdom of established institutions. According to him these established institutions are not invented by anybody; and they are not made also. As days passed far reaching developments took place in them. Since they grow they must be approached with reverence. Because of experience, familiarity and respect for them the old institutions work well. They are better and fitter for the people. They are very useful for the smooth functioning of government. From the above views of Burke, it is very clear that he was staunch supporter of conservation.

Burke was an anti-revolutionary. He opposed revolutions and condemned French Revolution. He thought that French Revolution was a damnable and dangerous one. He considered that the destruction of ancient political, religious, social and economic institutions was due to the wrath against conservatism. Since he belongs to the conservative tradition he profoundly and eloquently expressed in the "Reflections on French Revolution" his deep horror of such revolutionary methods.

Another evident to indicate his conservative policy is his views regarding the origin of the state. According to Locke the state was the product of social contract, for Burke it is a convention of slow organic growth.

Another example for his conservative policy was his faith in Divine will. He was a great religious minded man. He was of the opinion that religion is the foundation of State. The same religion is the basis for the creation of civil society. Apart from this it is the sole and whole source of all good and comfort. Hence he put more stress on religion. According to him the existence of church was itself an expression of nationhood as well as its consecration. He further said that every individual was very essential for good citizenship.

Burke had high regard for the British Constitution. He had full of praise and high esteem over the constitution. The British constitution was a natural growth. One of the most significant and salient features of the constitution is its principle of checks and balances. It afforded, he thought real protection to the liberty and property because they were not mere hypothesis but established rule of action.

Burke disfavoured the idea of popular sovereignty. He opposed the redistribution of seats and universal suffrage. He also denied equality of political rights to the people. In one of his works his attitude towards the English political institutions was expressed thus, "We fear God — We look with awe to the King; with affection to Parliament, with duty to magistrate, with reverence to priest and with respect to nobility." From his statement it is very obvious that he cherished and nourished the flourished old institutions. The people of England had great regard towards their King. Even now show their respect to the King (Queen). They have imposed their affection to their Parliament. They are very dutiful towards their magistrates. The priests and nobles are reverenced and respected by the people of England.

Burke was not a democrat. According to him democratic principles are not useful for the stability of a Government. He was convinced that stability and greatness of a nation depended upon the existence of a strong and powerful aristocracy. It itself is clear evident for his conservatism. According to John Bowle, "He is indeed the greatest prophet of English Conservatism." The statement of John Bowle out and out suitable for Burke. The view of John Bowle is shared by Hearnshaw when he comments about Burke that, "He was always a reformer and never a revolutionary, always a Conservative and never a Tory".

Burke as reformers : Edmund Burke is one of the most well known figures in English history. He was a sincere statesman; a prominent political thinker; an excellent orator. He played an important role in all major political issues for about 30 years after 1765, and remains an important figure in the history of political thought. He is rated as one of the world's greatest orators.

Edmund Burke was made private secretary to Lord Rockingham, a Whig leader. Burke continued in the same position till 1782. In 1774 he was elected a member of Parliament for Bristol. He was not able to win the confidence of his constituents. Then he served for sometime as a member of Melton. He gave the most famous statement on the role of the member of Parliament during his stay at Bristol. Burke remarked that member should be representative not a delegate.

Burke did not hesitate to criticise the bad measures of George III. He published a pamphlet in 1770 i.e., his "Thoughts on the causes of the Present discontents." In it he condemned and criticised the attempt of George III to revive some of the royal powers which had lost some influence in the reigns of the first two Georges. Further he offered in his pamphlet the precise definition of party and its aims and objects. According to him political party as body of men should be united on public principle and it could act as a constitutional link between king and Parliament. Later on in 1780 and 1781 he actively took part in regulating the Civil List. These events clearly indicate his political enthusiasm and earnestness.

No doubt Burke was a politician. This is amply shown by his varied participation of events connected with the American Revolution, Irish Question, the misdeeds and mismanagement of the East India Company and the French Revolution. With the result he made many marvellous contributions by way of writing books connected with these events. Those writings are called political writings of Burke.

According to Burke rights exist only in the state and not outside the state. If there is no state there can be no rights. In addition to this he claims that civil rights should be extended to all whereas the political rights should be given only to those who are having the capacity to enjoy and ability to exercise the rights.

A great issue which confronted Burke in 1765 was the conflict with the American Colonies. During the American War of Independence, he gave wholehearted support for the colonies in the Parliament. One of the most important drastic steps taken by the mother country was the enforcement of Stamp Act. It was not only damnable but also dangerous one. In 1776 he spoke for the repeal of the Stamp Act on a concession to American colonies. At the same time he did not hesitate to support the Declaratory Act which gave the Constitutional right to his country to tax the colonists. Hence he made two best known speeches in the Parliament viz., "On American Taxation" (1774) and "On Moving his Resolutions for conciliation with America" (1775).

During this time in Ireland also the government had enforced injurious trade restrictions. Moreover the government violated the civil rights. Burke was always very sympathetic towards Ireland. Hence in the Parliament he pleaded for the freedom of Ireland. For this also he can be rightly called a politician rather than a political philosopher.

Similarly Burke had taken interest in the affairs of India also. At this juncture the East India Company had created an extensive Empire. Burke opposed the interference of the British Government in the Affairs of the Company. But he did not ask the abandonment of British rule in India. The only thing he insisted was that the imperial power must be based on moral code. So far as Indian affair is concerned he made two best known speeches namely "On Mr. Fox's East India Bill" and "On the Nabob of Arcot's debts" in 1783 and 1785 respectively.

Another important political activity of Burke was his attitude towards Warren Hastings. He was dead against Warren Hastings. Warren Hastings was the then Governer-General of India i.e. 1773-1785. Burke regarded Hastings as the tyrant of Britain in India. Due to the instigation and initiation of Burke the impeachment of Hastings was brought in 1787. Burke spoke in the Parliament in connection with the impeachment of Hastings that Britain must be in India for India's sake and Indians' benefit or nor at all.

In spite of enormous criticisms and faults and failings of Hastings the impeachment failed in the House of Lords. Burke also failed to make the institution of impeachment a regular practice of free government. This itself is an evident to show that he was a politician.

Burke vehemently condemned the French Revolution. He described it as a strange and nameless catastrophe. In his greatest work "Reflections on the Revolution in France." He discussed the actual course of revolution, examining the personalities, motives and policies of its leaders. According to him the cause of the revolution was the revolutionists. He opposed the revolution to the end of his life.

Burke was the founder of conservation. But there were signs of liberalism also. He was not a democrat. His theory of representation is very clearly expressed in his own words, "Parliament is not a Congress of ambassadors from different hostile interest but parliament is a deliberative body of one nation, with one interest that of the whole. "The members of Parliament must oppose particular interests which offend general interests." From the above facts it is very obvious that "Burke was a politician but not a political philosopher."

■■

XI

Thomas Paine (1737–1809)

Early Career : Thomas Paine was born on 29th January, 1737 at Thetford in Norfolk. He was a Quaker by birth. Since his parent were very poor, he could not get a systematic education. He spent his early days as a sailor; teacher and exerciseman. During his early days he was confronted with miseries and misfortunes and sorrow and sufferings due to the difficulties and hardships. The death of his wife, his unhappy second marriage and his sufferings in life created in him the sympathy for poor and the downtrodden.

Thomas Paine was influenced by two persons. John Wilkes and Benjamin Franklin who were mainly responsible for his great political career. He joined the Headstrong Club at Lewis in 1768. During this time Paine was very much influenced by Wilke's writings.

On the advice of Benjamin Franklin, the American Agent in London. Paine left for America in 1774. Paine became an editor of the Pennsylvania Magazine in U.S.A. and remained there for eighteen months in this capacity. There he published his first pamphlet "Common sense" on July 4, 1776. This influenced the colonists to clamour more for their liberation and independent from the Yoke of British imperialism. The common sense swept through colonies made its deep impression the American mind, and drove public opinion toward the final break with Britain.

His Works : Pamphlets like "The Crisis", "The Public Good", and "The Right of Man" are best examples of Paine's constructive philosophy. In 1786 he published his "Dissertations on Government; the Affairs of the Bank; and Paper Money." He attacked Pitt's war policy in his "Prospects on the Rubicon", published in 1780. In 1792 he also published his letter "Addressed to the Addressers on the Late Proclamation", inciting the British people to form a republic. The Rights of Man and Address greatly offended the British Government. Hence he was outlawed from that country.

In France he attacked the policy of the revolutionaries particularly the execution of Louis XVI. Consequently he was expelled from France. During this time he published his, "The Age of Reason" in France which started trouble in America. In 1796 he published the "Decline and Fall of the English System of Finance" and "Letter to Washington". He died on 8th June, 1809 at the age of seventy two in New York.

His views : Paine's constructive political philosophy is chiefly found in his two famous pamphlets "Common Sense" and "The Rights of Man." The fundamental basis of his political doctrine is his idea of Society and State. Man is free and gregarious by nature according to Paine. He satisfies his wants with the help of others. He is not able to achieve anything alone. In the circumstances stated above the man was forced to form the society in the beginning. Due to the anomaly and animosity men failed to live peacefully. It necessitated them to form the government later on by a group of men through a contract. So Paine says, "Society is produced by our wants, and government by our wickedness; the former promoted our happiness positively, by uniting our affections, the later negatively by restraining our vices. The first is a patron the last a punisher" (Common sense-Page 1). The above difference between State and Society made by Paine is clearly derived from the philosophy transmitted by Locke.

According to Paine society is a blessing one for every state whereas government is necessary evil. Every man should act according to his conscience. If he did so no law would be necessary. If he did not respect his conscience a government became necessary to make and enforce laws in the society. Since man did not like to lose all liberty, he agreed to create or form a government by sacrificing some of his liberty. From this we know the basic function of government is to ensure his freedom by giving security. According to him the government must be responsible and limited.

Regarding sovereignty he says that it belongs to the people. He further adds that "every citizen is a member of the sovereignty and as such can acknowledge no personal subjection; and disobedience can be only to the laws." Again he says that "nation is essentially the source of all sovereignty, not can any individual, or anybody of men, be entitled to any authority which is not expressly derived from it." So his sovereignty resembles to that of Rousseau's General will.

From Paine's writings we know the vivid description of various types of government. Out and out he was a republican. He divides the government into four types viz. democracy, aristocracy, monarchy and republic. According to him monarchy and aristocracy represent the corrupt form. They are based on ignorance. Democracy is inadequate to the affairs of an extensive population. Representative Government is the only logical and adequate system. Paine favours the republican form of government because it is built upon universal suffrage and run by representatives elected by the nation. He condemns the British monarchical system and speaks in high praise of a republic as that of America.

Another feature of his philosophy is the conception of rights. According to him "all men are of one degree and consequently that all men are born equal and with equal natural rights." These words are seen in his "The Rights of Man" Part I. The natural rights of man are liberty, property, security and resistance to oppression. These natural rights are highly responsible for the foundation of civil rights. "The Rights of Man" has been compared to the "Ten Commandments". It is the duty of the government to preserve these rights surrendered by the individual and should not make inroad into these natural rights retained by him. In this way the rights of man serve as a sort of limitations on the government.

Paine then turns his attention towards the conception of Law. It is also another significant feature of his political philosophy. According to him, "all laws are acts, but all acts are not laws." He points out that by no means all the enactments of a legislature are entitled to the name and character of law.

Lastly, it is also significant to note his views on the form and content of the written constitution. He calls the English political system as defective one. Written constitutions could alone secure the natural rights and popular liberty from being encroached upon by government. R.C. Gupta says that "according to Paine a constitution was not an ideal but a fact. It must be visible. A constitution is antecedent to government. The latter is a creature of the former." The constitution is made by the people and not by the government. If we go through the English constitution, we cannot find the above facts in it. Hence England has no constitution at all.

Paine's enthusiasm is seen in favouring the American Constitution. He says "the American constitutions were to liberty what grammar is to language". He further adds, "They define its parts of speech and practically construct them into syntex." At the same time he could not agree with the American constitutionalists with regard to the theory of separation of powers. According to him there are only two kinds of power. They are making and executing of laws.

Like Mahatma Gandhi, Paine was a great humanitarian. He regarded all of humanity as his country and thought of himself as a universal man. Since he suffered a lot in his early days he was always sympathetic towards the poor and the downtrodden. According to R.C. Gupta "he had enrolled under the banner of freedom and remained its Royal and energetic apostle to his last day. In its name he had helped to create one country, the United States, played a large role in the life of another, France and left his deep mark on still a third England". He had won in his life time enduring name and fame without any formal education. He had stirred and stimulated the hearts and awaken and shaken the minds of his contemporaries as few men achieved in their life and earned himself a permanent place in the annals of history.

XII

Jeremy Bentham (1748–1832)

Jeremy Bentham was the founder of utilitarianism. He was born in London on February 15, 1748. He was the son of Jeremiah Bentham, who was a lawyer. His father wanted his son also be a lawyer. He obtained a great reputation for Greek and Latin verse writing when he was at Westminster school. In 1760, he went to Queen's College, Oxford where he acquired a thorough acquaintance with Robert Sanderson's logic. Then he went to Lincoln's Inn in England for Pegal in 1763. His mind was learned towards scientific experiments and hence he could not succeed in the legal side. Since, he found the work dull, gave up the same. From the beginning he was interested more in the defects of the legal system than in mastering its details. He was delicate, nervous and precocious.

Bentham went to Russia in 1785 to see his brother. His brother was an engineer and was employed for the creation of a modern Agricultural and Industrial colony in the Ukraine. In 1792, the National Assembly of France conferred on him the title of a French citizen.

Bentham was the chief promotor of the University College, London, which was founded in 1827. From a small college, it developed into the largest University of commonwealth.

Bentham was very lucky in having a large number of persons as his collaborators and disciples. His first and foremost disciple was James Mill. Sir Samuel Romilly, a distinguished lawyer, David Ricardo, the great economist, J.S. Mill, a great philosopher, John Austin and George Grote the prominent figures were some of his friends. Lord Shellbourn the distinguished Whig leader, who was the Prime Minister of England in 1782-83 was a friend of Bentham.

Bentham was a great writer. He published as many as 30 works during his life time. Nearly 20 works were published posthumously. We find in his writings law, political economy, education, church, language, poor law, local government, banking social service, census, international organisation etc. Among them "Fragment on Government" was his first book published in 1776. It may be said to mark the beginning of philosophic radicalism. His other important works were "Defence of Usury", "Introduction to the Principles of Morals and Legislation", "Emancipate your Colonies", "Essay on Political Tactics", "Principles of International Law", "Manual of Political Economy" and "Church of England". In 1809, he wrote his "A Catechism of Parliamentary Reform". In it, he pleaded for annual elections, equal electoral constituencies, wide suffrage and secret ballot.

Bentham's sole insistence was on the principle of utility by which he meant "the greatest good of the greatest number" was based on the end of the state. There is more truth than exaggeration in the words that Hazlitt wrote of him as late as 1825 — "His name is little known in England, better in Europe and best of all in the plains of Chilli and the mines of Mexico. He has offered constitutions for the new world and legislated for future times..."

Bentham lived upto eighty two. He worked very hard till the end of his life. He himself said that he worked "Eodifying like any Dragon." His ambition had been no small one. J.B. the most ambitious of the ambitious" he wrote. He died happy in the thought that the ambition was well on the way to being realised. According to Leslie Stephen "he is said to have expressed the wish that he could awaken once in a century to contemplate the prospect of a world gradually adopting his principles and so making steady progress in happiness and wisdom."

J.S. Mill says, "A place therefore must be assigned to Bentham among the masters of wisdom, the great teachers and permanent intellectual ornaments of human race ..." The service of Bentham to political thought was enormous and also excellent. In the words of Doyle, "Jeremy Bentham stood out as the dominating philosopher of the readical group." He further says that "he was inductive scientist drawing conclusions from his laboriously collected data." Referring to the death of Bentham in his ripe age of 84 the same writer remarks that he died, "Venerated by a group of disciples as a patriarch, a spiritual leader, almost a God, with James Mill as his Saint Paul."

Bentham, the English utilitarian philosopher was one of the principal influences on the reforming thought of the 19th century. He was primarily a legal reformer. Coleridge once said that "until we understand a man's ignorance we are ignorant of his understanding." Hence C.L. Wayper says "Bentham was not an outstanding philosopher though paradoxically he occupies an important place in the history of philosophy....He took his theory of knowledge from Locke and Hume, the pleasure and pain principle from Helvetius, the notion of sympathy and antipathy from Hume, the idea of utility from any of half a score of writers.....".

Although Bentham wrote on the various aspects of the political state of his day, his distinctive field was Ethics and Jurisprudence. So the English men are greatly indebted to Jeremy Bentham.

Principle of Utility : The moral and political philosophy of Bentham is based on his doctrine of utility. In the "Fragment, on Government" published in 1776, he preached the principle of the greatest happiness of the greatest number. The whole structure of his utilitarian theory rests on his assumption that "Nature has placed mankind under two sovereign masters pain and pleasure." To seek pleasure and avoid pain is the tendency of the human beings. Everything that brings happiness is good, he tells us and nothing that does not bring happiness is good.

According to Bentham pleasure and pain supplied the motive force to the activities of man. Every man tried to get pleasure and avoid pain. The doctrine of utility therefore is a hedonistic doctrine. While describing the good and bad consequences of an action, he simply meant the happy or painful consequences of an action. Here he accepted that all ideas are derived from the senses.

Pleasures are simply individual sensations. But Happiness is not merely the individual sensation; it is a state of mind, a bundle of sensations. Every pleasure he tells is a prima facie good and ought to be pursued. But happiness is not the piling up of all pleasures. It is the net result — i.e it sometimes entails the rejection of some pleasures indulgence in which would have painful consequences. It is on the basis of pain and pleasure that a man performs any action in his life. He calls this principle of pain and pleasure the principle of utility.

According to Bentham the pleasure and pain depend upon the actions of the individuals. If their actions are right, they would promote their happiness. If their actions are wrong they would promote their unhappiness. When applied to political science, it referes to measures of government. Those measurers of government are right which further the happiness of the community. It is the duty of the government to further the happiness of the community. Indeed the government should increase the happiness of the individual. At the same time it is very difficult for any government to promote the happiness of every individual of the community. Hence the aim of the government should be the promotion of the greatest happiness of the greatest number.

Further Bentham is very particular in mentioning the quantity of the happiness rather than its quality. According to him pleasure and pain could be measures through these factors like *intensity* i.e. depth of feeling *duration, certainty, propinquity* i.e. pleasure which is nearer fecundity i.e. pleasure which is followed by a chance of being accompanied by sensations of the same kind is greater than otherwise *purity* and *extensiveness*. The extensiveness is concerned with the number of persons who are affected by them. In this connection he says that it is the foremost duty of the legislators to classify those pleasures. He himself enumerates fourteen simple pleasures and twelve simple pains. They are sense, wealth, skill, amity, good name, power, piety, benevolence, malevolence, memory, imagination, expectation, association and relief. The pains are privation, sense awkwardness, enmity, ill name, piety, benevolence, malevolence, imagination, expectation, memory and association. These pleasures and pains govern all our ideas and all our actions, whatever they may be. Pleasures and pains are further subdivided into two parts viz. self-regarding and others regarding. Only benevolence and malevolence were others regarding.

One of the seven factors mentioned above for the measurement of pleasures and pains is extensiveness or the number of persons affected. The value of thing is more or less according to the number of persons taking part in pleasure or pain. Here it depends upon their action as stated above.

According to the doctrine of utility every person is to be permitted to pursue his own way of happiness. Eventhough it may be a perverted pleasure the sage feels happiness in asceticism. From this, it is clear that every individual will seek pleasure and avoid pain and that every person is the best judge of his own happiness. On the contrary, the principle of utility presupposes that the moral standard of man's action is to be judged from the quantity of general happiness it can produce.

It goes without saying that the principle of the greatest good of the greatest number immensely affected the legislation not only in the 19th century but also in the present century. It gave the politicians and statesmen a measuring rod by which they could judge the utility or otherwise of particular piece of legislation. Although the Benthamite doctrine is narrow and psychologically false "It has an immense value because it denied the infallibility of the supreme person who endeavours to foist his own morality or his own type of happiness upon others whom he believes to be the pitiful dupes of ignorance", according to Ivor Brown.

The principle of utility of Bentham has been severely and seriously criticised from many directions. Firstly, his base materialism is denounced by Moralists and idealists. Secondly, there is no such thing as a moral or an immoral action as Bentham says. Thirdly, it is very difficult to measure pleasure and pain. It may differ from person to person. The highest aim of the government is to augment the sum total of human happiness and diminish unhappiness.

Bentham applied this principle of utility to state, sovereignty, natural rights, law, punishment and government. In spite the many criticisms levelled against his abstract theory, Bentham has won a prominent place in the history of democratic thoughts and political theory. Even with his limitations, he has been able to preach a message of humanism.

His views on state : Jeremy Bentham is considered as the greatest exponent of utilitarian philosophy. The utilitarian philosophy occupied a prominent place during the 19th century. The utilitarian explanation of the state is not only an explanation in terms of an unlimited end, but also in terms of the particular character of the state which differentiates it from man's other activitics. A theory which maintains that the end of the state is the promotion of utility simply identified thc end of the state with the end of human life. Yet clearly the state has a particular part to play in human life. The utilitarians including Bentham tell us in what way the state is peculiar, it is the sole source of law, which is the most certain of the four 'sanctions' or overriding motives which govern the lives of men. These are the *physical sanction* which operates in the ordinary course of nature; the *moral sanction* which arises from the general feeling of society; the *religious sanction* which is applied by the immediate hand of a superior invisible being, either in the present life or in a future" and the *political sanction* which operates through government and the necessity for which is the explanation of the state.

According to Bentham, the state is primarily a law making body by a group of persons organised for the promotion and maintenance of happiness and acting through law to that end. He argues that the state's supreme power is unlimited and absolute in so far as it does not undermine the value of utility. Within the framework of utility, the state can makc and unmake any law and no limits can be set to its authority or power. This supreme power of the state is the source of all laws. These laws are made by the state to promote the happiness of the people.

According to Bentham, law should fulfil five important

conditions. They are (i) it should ensure an efficient government, (ii) it must ensure inexpensive justice without inordinate delay, (iii) it must be comprehensive, (iv) it must be uniform, and (v) it should make justice predictable and it should answer the needs of the people. If the above conditions are fulfilled the law would be the fittest and suitable instrument to promote human happiness or utility.

2. *Punishment* : Bentham gives a fine place for the theory of punishment and prison reforms in his political philosophy. According to him the chief end of punishment is to prevent crime. It should not be merely vindictive. Exactly it should be suited to the purpose. Again it should be neither more or less. It should secure the good of the community. If there is any necessity for capital punishment it should be given otherwise not. The welfare of society should be the measuring rod. Moreover, the criminal or the offender should be punished in public so that the others may be frightened.

According to him certain principles should be followed in fixing the punishment according to offence. They are (i) The quantity of the punishments should be differed according to offence, (ii) The punishment should be equable neither lead to unnecessary pain nor should it be inefficaious, (iii) All similar offences should be punished alike, (iv) Punishment should create an example and serve as deterrent, (v) punishment should par-take of the nature of the offence, (vi) It should rest on the principle of frugality, (vii) It should be a reformation to the criminal, (viii) It should diable him or prevent him from repeating the crime in future, (ix) It should compel the offender as far as possible to compensative those injured by the offence, (x) Punishment should meet popular approval and should not excite sympathy for the offender, and (xi) The punishment should always be remissible. From the above principles it is very obvious that Bentham was very sympathetic towards the criminals and he stood for the improvement of the lot of the criminals.

3. *Prison Reform*: Bentham believed that a great many criminals and evil doers could be restored to society as useful and

self respecting members. On the belief he advocated many salient reforms for the reformation of the criminal and for the teaching of industries while in confinement. He put forth a plan called "*Panopticon*" for the regular supervision of the daily life of the convicts. He described Panopticon as a mill grinding rogus honest and idle men industrious. The building i.e. the model prison was a circular glass roofed tank like structure with cells along the external wall facing toward a central rotunda which made it possible for its officers stationed in the rotunda to keep all the inmates (Convicts) under constant and continuous surveillence. The criminals were to be taught useful trades, elementary education, moral and religious ideas. On their release they were to be given employment. He spent lot of money for the same. But he failed in his attempt. Later on some of his reforms were carried out.

4. *Natural rights, individualism and theory of Government* : Bentham criticises the idea of natural rights. Natural Rights says Bentham are "simple nonsense; natural and imprescriptible rights rhetorical nonsense — nonsense upon stills". For him natural law and natural rights are meaningless. He substitutes for them the principle of utility.

Like Paine, Rousseau and Locke he has been considered as an individualist. The primary aim of Bentham is to promote the welfare of the community. To quote him, "The community is a fictious body composed of the individual persons who are considered as constituting as it were its members. It is vain to talk of the interest of the community without understanding what is the interest of the individual. A thing is said to promote the interest or to be for the interest of an individual when it tends to aid to the sum total of his pleasures or what comes to the something to diminish the sum total of his pains."

Bentham stands for free government on the basis of the principle of utility. He tries to differentiate it from a despotic rule. He is in favour of a unicameral legislature elected every year on the basis of adult franchise. A free government is always responsible and accountable for its conduct and policies to the governed. Free government provides the free press and freedom of association. Bentham regards democracy as the best form of government to promote the greatest happiness of the greatest number. But he says that direct democracy is not possible since its representatives may be kept under constant control by enforcing such constitutional safeguards as universal suffrage, annual parliaments, vote by ballot, election of the Prime Minister by the parliament, the recruitment of civil service by competitive examinations. All are equal before the eye of law and the equal distribution of wealth are other basic principles for the representative form of government.

5. *Justice*: Bentham is considered as a great law reformer. He criticises the legal system of England. He is of the opinion that knowledge of the laws of the country should be within the reach of the people. For that purpose, law must be expressed in plain words and short sentences. Further he finds fault with the drafting and the style of the laws of his country. The system of administration of Justice is also not satisfactory there according to Bentham. He condemns the insuperable difficulties that were placed in the way of the litigants to get justice. So Bentham wrote thus "In this country justice is sold and dearly sold and it is denied to him who cannot disburse the price at which it is purchased."

6. *Education*: Bentham is considered a fore-runner in the field of educational reforms. He believes that mankind can be improved with the help of education. Bentham says that it is the duty of the state to look after the education of the poor children. For that purpose he suggests certain reforms in the administration of poor law. It is a matter of common knowledge that his views have been accepted and adopted in every progressive country of the world today.

7. *Church*: Bentham criticises the church of England for its sinecure offices. He regards the clergymen as the enemies of progress. He is sceptical with regard to religion as that hinders intellectual progress by supporting belief apart from experience "it is only safe ground." His conclusion is, that religion is useless and harmful.

8. *Liberty and equality*: Bentham's theory of rights is based

on three principles i.e. (i) the rights are enforceable, (ii) the rights and duties are inseparable, and (iii) rights are not considered as postulates of liberty. Law does not aim at liberty. The aim of the government is happiness and not liberty. Liberty is not an important part of happiness. If the object of the state is security, security leads to equality. To Bentham equality cannot be an absolute one; it runs counter to utility. He is not for absolute equality. But he is of the opinion that men are born equal to be happy.

9. *Reforms* : Bentham is styled as a great reformer. The number of practical reforms which he advocated are a legion. The principal among them as given by Davidson are; the reform of corrupt and restricted parliamentary systems; a thorough going municipal reform; the humanitarian of the terribly cruel criminal law of the time; the improvement of prisons and prison management; the abolition of imprisonment for debt; the elimination of usury laws; the repeal of religious test; the reform of the poor laws; the suppression of "sturdy beggars", the utilisation of able bodied paupers, the training of pauper children, the establishment of a vast scheme of national education; the institution of "frugality banks" (Savings Banks) and friendly societies; the forming of code for merchant shipping; the protection of inventors; the encouragement of local courts; comprehensive system of health legislation; the creation of the public prosecutors and of advocates of the poor; a thorough going revision of hereditary rights; the supervision of scientific and philosophical foundation and the recall of public officials." Many of his reforms have since been incorporated into the laws of various countries. Hence, Sir Henry Maine paid a glowing tribute to Bentham in the following manner, "I do not know a single law reform effected since Bentham's day which cannot be traced to his influence."

■■

XIII

Johann Goltlieb Fichte (1762–1814)

Early Life : Johann Goltlieb Fichte was a great German philosopher. He expounded the theory of ethical idealism. He gave special attention to socialism and to German nationalism. He was born in Saxony in 1762. His father was a weaver. He studied in the universities of Jena and Leipzig from 1780 to 1784. His special subjects were theology and philosophy. Then he left the university campus and went to Prussia. There he mingled with the people and shared their miseries of the Napoleonic conquest. Later on he became a professor in the newly established University of Berlin. This period marked the height of his philosophical development and the publication of his most important technical works. Unfortunately, this period ended in disaster and despair. His philosophy which identified God with the moral order was taken by many to be virtually atheistic. As a result he resigned the post in 1799. Then he turned his attention towards publishing his popular works.

His works : J.G. Fichte published "The Vocation of Man" in 1800. In 1806 he published his another work, "The Characteristics of the Present Age." In the same year his another work, "The Way to the Blessed Life" was released for reading. In 1808 he published the "Addresses to the German Nation." His important works are "Theory of State" and "Closed Commercial State." Fichte gave an elaborate theory of state socialism and national state. In his famous address to the German people he put forth an exalter conception of the character and mission of the Germans. No wonder he advocated the ideal of German only.

His political ideas : The philosophy of Fichte was the first of the idealist systems derived from Kant, which made Germany the centre of European philosophical activity in the early 19th century. He was much under the influence of Rousseau. He wrote thus, "Peace be on Rousseau's ashes and blessings in his memory; for he was kindled fire in many souls". Again "My system from beginning to end is nothing but an analysis of the concept of freedom."

According to Fichte, there was no such thing as a pre-social state of nature in which people enjoyed certain natural rights "The state itself is man's natural condition" as viewed by him. He gave importance to only one natural right i.e. the absolute right of the person to be in the world of sense only cause and never effect."

Regarding social contract Fichte referred to three kinds of contracts, viz., property contract, protection contract and the union contract. He defined the property contract as rights of free action in the world sense. Property contract fixed the bouny bary to the property of each. According to this contract every individual gave up his claim to what lay outside a certain sphere on the condition that all gave up their claims to what lay within that sphere. By the protection contract, every individual agreed to contribute his share of force necessary for the maintenance of the partitions made by the property contract. By the union contract every individual agreed with every other individual to unite into a whole for the effective accomplishment of the ends involved in the previous two contracts. This contract completed the social pact and constituted a sovereign.

As regards the functions of the state, Fichte rejected the idea that the end of the "state was" to make happy, rich, healthy, orthodox, virtuous and God willing saved eternally." Nor it was merely to preserve and protect each in his personal rights and his property. The function of the state according to him was "to give to each for the first time in his own, to instal him for the first time in his property and then first to protect him in it." It was the duty of the state to give proper aids to all sections of people. The state was to distribute proportionately the raw materials and finished products of the country. Again it was to fix the prices of various commodities. It was the duty of the state to carry on all the foreign trade. He stood for the economic self sufficiency of every state. Commercial rivalries were responsible for war. Fichte too like Kant had the ideal of a world league of nations.

According to Fichte, natural boundaries should be preserved. Nature indicated the geographical basis of every state.

Fichte held that a government might be monarchic or aristocratic, elective or hereditary but never democratic. Because the whole people can never take part in the governmental work. Fichte said that the right of final Judgment upon the conduct of the government must be with the people as a whole. He suggested an institution known as Ephorate whose duty was to watch any violation of the constitution and to provide the machinery, when necessary for the expression of the sovereign will of the people. If this check on the government failed, the people as a whole had the right of revolution. Dunning remarks thus "such was Fichte's contribution to the solution of the much debated problem, how to keep the government in accord with the constitution without permitting any branch of the government to shape the constitution on its will."

Catlin calls him as one of the fathers of fascism. Reinhold Aris says Fichte was the first thinker in Germany who developed a consistent system of liberalism. According to Catlin, "The German Rousseau, humanised cosmopolitan anarchist liberal, liberal socialist, collectivist national, national socialist, the agony of Fichte's doubts and changes expresses more clearly than it is expressed in any other writer the crisis in civilisation for this age."

■■

XIV
George Wilhelm Frederick Hegel (1770–1831)

C.L. Wayper writes in his "Political Thought" that "The most outstanding advocate of the organic theory of the State and one of the most important and influential thinkers of modern history was Hegel. He was born in Stuttgart in Wurtemberg in Southern Germany in 1770. His father was a civil servant. In his school days he was very bright and brilliant and hence he became a school prize winner. Then he studied theology in the University of Tabingen. He fell under the spell of the French Revolution in his youth and declared it as "a glorious mental dawn." During this time he was very thorough with the writings of Rousseau. He worked as a private tutor for sometime. There he wrote the life of Jesus Christ.

After serving as a private tutor for some years he became lecturer in the university of Jena in 1801. During this time Kant exercised a tremendous influence over Hegel. But Hegel never was a Kantian. The contract between Kant and Hegel is considerably greater than that between Plato and Aristotle.

In 1806, Jena fell before the victorious armies of Napoleon. As a result of this Hegel had to leave that place. After Jena, Hegel worked as a local editor and also became a school headmaster in Nuremberg. He published his three volume work on the "Science of Logic." Because of this work, he became the most loudly acclaimed of German philosophers. He became a professor at Heidelberg university in 1816. He was then 47 years old. Here he wrote his "Encyclopaedia of the Philosophical Sciences", the fullest treatment of his general philosophical system that he ever produced.

Hegel then shifted to Berlin University where he accepted the chair of Philosophy. While at Berlin he acted as the official philosopher of Prussia. In this capacity he expounded the nature of knowledge, god, universe and the state. Hence his ideas had tremendous effect both upon theoretical and practical politics. He made world history culminate in Hohen-zollern Prussia. At Berlin Hegel did not consider himself under any obligation to enter into the conflicts of the politicians. He criticised the English Parliamentary Reform movement which was responsible for the passing of the Reform Act of 1832. Hegel died of cholera at the age of 61. He was buried next to Fichte.

The Philosophy of Hegel is to be found in his works "The Phenomenology of Spirit", "Logic", "The Philosophy of Right" and the "Philosophy of History."

Hegel represents the climax of German idealism in political thought. Like Kant and Fichte, Hegel too based his political system of psychology i.e. on the conception of positive and self determining freedom. He combined the historical sense of Vico and Montesquieu with the philosophic eminence of Kant and Fichte in his writings. The corner stone of his philosophy is evolution, the evolution of ideas by dialectical process.

According to Prof. Sabine the significance of the political thought of Hegel centres round two points and those are the dialectic as a method and the idealisation of the nation state. These two points became the source of the two most important stands of later political thought.

The concept of Geist was basic in all the political thinking of Hegel. It appeared in many aspects namely Weltgeist (World spirit) Volksgeist (National Spirit) and Zeitgeist (Time Spirit). It dominated Hegel's idea of historical evolution.

Vaughan has pointed out to the various contribution made by Hegel in his philosophy. In this connection it is pointed out that Hegel grasped the connection between morals and politics and handled the same with a far greater insight, than any of his predecessors. During the 19th century Hegel was hailed not merely as the official philosopher of Prussia but also as the philosopher of the age in the same way Aristotle and St. Thomas Aquinas were regarded as the philosophers of their times.

Hegel remarked that the function of philosophy was merely to explain and not to create. According to Prof. Sabine "The philosophy of Hegel aimed at nothing less than a complete and systematic reconstruction of modern thought....." C.L. Wayper says, "Hegel's great influence on philosophy, on political philosophy, on politics is not then to be denied. Unfortunately, he is as difficult to understand as he is important Language has frequently been accorded pride of place among the major arts of deception."

The Hegelian theory of the state leads to state absolutism, totalitarianism and nationalism and goes against the modern nations of liberty and democracy. His idolising of the state has led to Fascism. His dialectics modified by the materialism of Marx has resulted in communism. Hegel was wrong in identifying the state with society. There is no doubt that Hegel, in spite of many short. comings in his philosophy was one of the greatest philosophers of the world. One may be critic of Hegel and Hegelian heritage but one cannot gainsay its universal importance.

His Dialectic Method : According to William Ebenstein "In the German intellectual tradition, Hegel's system of philosophy towards over the rest in more than one way. Hegel's work enompasses philosophy metaphysics, religion, art, ethics, history and politics. In its range alone his work is unique in Germany and possibly in the whole world."

According to Hegel, the progress of human civilisation has not been in a positive straight line. It was in a zig zag sort of movement. The main aim of philosophy was to know nature and the entire words of experience and to comprehend the reason for it. The world is essentially a dynamic and it is not static. The true concept must be an active moving process, of evolution. In the process of evolution, something that is undeveloped gets developed by splitting up, assuming many different and opposing forms. It then unites or combines again in a new concrete objects and becomes a unity in diversity. The higher state in the process of evolution is the realisation of the lower. The lower form is negatived in the higher. It gets carried over or sublimated. The whole process of evolution was given the name of Dialectic by Hegel. The term 'dialectic' was first used by the Sophists and other Greek thinkers. According to them, it was the method of disputation to show that the statement of a speaker was self refuting. According to Plato "the Dialectic was a process of thinking by which the dramatic conflict of ideas was determined by definition."

According to Hegel, the dialectic was not merely a process by which logical ideas developed. It was a method or process by which all idea in the world developed. History showed a continuous and orderly development. Hegel in and through his dialectic propounded the belief that reality could only be apprehended by a method of contrasting one thing with its opposite. Thus goodness was only understood when it was contrasted with badness, heat with cold, want with society. To Hegel, the real was the rational and the rational was the real.

The universe of known experience was in constant flux. It was moving towards a definite point. There was imminent necessity for the ends and purposes of that evolution. The whole process of evolution was governed by definite rational principles of thesis, antithesis and synthesis. According to him, we begin with an abstract universal concept called thesis; the concept gives rise to contradiction called antithesis; the contradictory concepts and reconciled in the third, called synthesis. It is the union of the other two concepts. Thus in the simple example of the evolution of the life germ in an egg the whole dialectic process could be seen. The egg contains a germ (thesis) which when fertilised gradually consumes (negatives) the contents of the egg. This act of destruction results not in death but in the production of a new form of life completely different in nature from its origin, the germ of its environment the contents. A chick (the synthesis of the two forces) emerges from the shell.

Hegel came forward to demonstrate that the laws of thought were similar to the laws of the universe. The thesis "despotism" will call into being democracy, the antithesis and form the clash between them the synthesis "constitutional monarchy" which contains the best of both results. The thesis, the family produces its antithesis, bourgeois society and from the resultant clash the synthesis the state emerges in which thesis and antithesis are raised to a higher power and reconciled.

Further Hegel distinguished between understanding and reason as did Carlyle. For him, "understanding was the mode of mind which seeks precision above all things and insists upon clear distinctions" Reason gives us a deeper insight into the real nature of things than understanding with its formal ratiocination. Apart from this, he differentiated the creative reason from reflective reason. According to him, creative reason was unconscious reason, reason unaware of itself — e.g. building up of family, society, state. Reflective reason reconstructs thought and by a conscious effort of thought the fabric which blinded by the very force of its creative power, it has ceased to recognise as its own.

Hegel also emphasised the need of history and tradition to solve the political and other problems. History is the process by which the spirit passes from knowing nothing to full knowledge of itself, the increasing revelation of the purposes of the Rational Mind. "The history of the world" therefore, says Hegel "presents us with a rational process." The Spirit on the way to its goal makes many experiments. The Spirit or the Reason does not know anything at the beginning of the world process. It develops slowly throughout the history of the world and ultimately reaches the truth Absolute. Hence it is said "the rational is the real and the real is the rational."

From the above theory of Hegel it is seen that the main purpose of Dialectic is to display historical necessity. Hegel used his dialectic theory for giving an explanation of the progress of society and its institutions. But he was not successful in his use of dialectic. In his philosophy of the Spirit, Hegel put forth his idea or notion of art, religion and philosophy in which he viewed the art as thesis, religion as antithesis and philosophy as synthesis. But it is not understandable in what sense religion is the opposite of art. It is not proper to say that both are related as germs and species or religion can be regarded as the differential. The fact is that Hegel's dialectic thrives on ambiguities of terminology.

According to Dr. Mc. Taggart though the dialectic method is wholly valid, its application in the explanation of various facts is questionable. First of all thesis, antithesis and synthesis cannot be recognised except in relation to one another. Secondly, in religion history, law and philosophy the dialectical process is affected by external influences. Thirdly, the application of this method to the field of natural and social sciences is intricated and not systematised.

1. *State*: Hegel's "Philosophy of Law" (Philosophic des Rechts) published in 1821, contains the best statements of his political ideas. In his "Philosophy of History" published posthumously in 1837 (six years after his death) Hegel defines the state as "the realisation of Freedom, the state exists for its own sake". Hegel puts more stress on the state and he regarded it as essentially divine in origin. Hence it must be looked with awe and reverence. He rejected the theory of social contract as the origin of the state. To Hegel the idea that men in the state of nature were free and equal appeared absurd and ridiculous. In the very beginning men lived as groups rather than as individuals. During the state of nature there was no equality or real freedom since the state was not originated by the voluntary union. He opined that the state was the product of a long process of evolution. It was not the creation of man at one time and place. Man being a social animal stated by Aristotle lived in groups even in a primitive state. First family came into existence. Out of the family the tribe developed and out of the tribe the state at first in a lower then in a higher form. Thus the first characteristic of the state of Hegel "Divine in Origin" is clearly indicated.

Another characteristic feature of the Hegelian state is the idea that the individual must be completely subordinated to the state, and the wishes and desires of the individual must be rejected in favour of the will of the state.

Another characteristic feature of the Hegelian state is that it was the embodiment of all reasons. It was the actualisation of freedom. It was rational in conception. The state was the incarnation of General will or the real will. True freedom for the individual consisted in obeying the laws of the state and cultivating "the everyday habit of looking on the commonwealth as our substantive purpose and the foundation of ourselves."

Hegel's State is absolute, omnipotent and infallible. The State is the march of God on earth. The state is God itself. It represented the last individual will. It has its own will and personality, superior to the wills and personalities of the individuals who formed it. As member of the state he had freedom in the state. The state was the creator of all rights and as such an individual had no rights against the state. It represented the unity of the universal and individual will. It was both objective and subjective freedom. In this way it was eternal.

The state also is an end in itself. It is not only the highest expression to which the spirit has yet attained, it is "the final embodiment of spirit on earth." There can be no spiritual evolution beyond the state. Similarly, there can be any more physical evolution beyond man.

Another characteristic feature of the state according to Hegel is society that must dominate mankind among the social institutions. It is higher and more important than the family, state is higher and more important than the society. Thus, he believed in the heirarchy of institutions.

2. *Freedom*: According to Hegel, the idea of freedom is the essence of man. The object of Hegel's theory of freedom was to remove the mistake of the French Revolution. In this sphere, he was no doubt indebted to Rousseau and Kant. But he thought Kantian freedom was negative limited and subjective. To him individual freedom was a social phenomenon. It was made possible in the moral life of the community. Freedom consisted in giving total obedience to the state and in the performance of one's duties.

3. *War*: According to Hegel, the state can make war in order to serve its interest. It should go to war in order to preserve its health and prevent corruption and decay. If there is no war for years together the health and strength of the state would definitely decline. He opposed to perpetual peace.

4. *International Law*: According to Hegel, the state was all powerful and absolute. Therefore, there was no such thing as international law which could bind the will of the state.

5. *Punishment*: On the basis of right and morality he discussed in detail the question of punishment. According to him, if a particular right was violated it was the duty of the state to punish the person who violated it. Punishment is a right both of the

society and the criminal. It should be given to the criminals, otherwise he would not be repeated.

6. *Property*: Hegel was in favour of private property. With the help of that private property, the individual can thrive himself. Without property there can be no progress in him.

7. *Constitution*: To Hegel, the state manifest itself in a constitution. There are three essential powers in the state viz. the legislative, the administrative and the monarchic. Among the three the monarchic power is the most important. It is the verifying force within the state. The first (legislative branch) is a thesis, the second (Administrative) is antithesis and the third (monarchic) is synthesis. The last one prevents the other two from disrupting the state. All other forms of government are regarded by Hegel as imperfect and useless.

As a philosophical conception sovereignty belongs to the state as a whole. As a result all are brought under the control of sovereignty. Further Hegel did not believe in revolutionary changes in the constitution. Institutions are not made in one day but grow gradually. Every institution is therefore rational even if it is imperfect. With the result of this they have a place in the dialectical movement.

8. *History*: According to Hegel, the course of history is governed by reason. Man plays a significant role in history. World history is the world judgement i.e. victory for one people and defeat for another. The course of history are determined by the process of eternal change. He says that the realisation of freedom is essential. This is the end of the world spirit as it moves toward absolute self consciousness. "It is the hub around with world history revolves. History is divided by going forward to this point and starting from it."

■■

XV

James Mill (1773–1836)

James Mill was born on 6th April, 1773 at Northwater Bridge in Forfarshire in Scotland. His father was a shoemaker and his mother was domestic servant of farming stock. He studied in the university of Edinburgh where he distinguished himself as a Greek scholar. He studied divinity and became a preacher in the church of Scotland. During this period he showed keen interest in the historical and philosophical studies.

James Mill went to London in 1802. There he devoted himself to journalism. He got temporary success in this field. He had nine children and J.S. Mill was the best of all. He had to work very hard for his livelihood.

James Mill published his first pamphlet on corn trade in 1804. From 1805 onwards he directed his attention towards literature. James Mill wrote many books. The most important of them are "History of India" published in three volumes in 1818. "Analysis of the Phenomena of the Human mind" published in 1829 and "Fragment of Makintosh" published in 1835. He wrote enormous articles. His most famous article was article on "Government" which was written by him in 1814. His other two authoritative articles were articles on "Jurisprudence" and "Law of Nations" in the Encyclopaedia Britannica.

James Mill's friendship with Jeremy Bentham exercised a tremendous influence upon him since 1808. Hence, he adopted Bentham's principles in his writings. The friendship between the two continued for the rest of their lives. Their relation was that of student and teacher. They were very near and dear each other from 1814 to 1817. James Mill and his wife lived with Bentham.

Even after leaving the residence of Bentham, he continued to have the same intimate relations with his master. He was the chief promoter of those principles. And more than anyone else it was Mill who opposed the beginnings of romanticism in the typical Benthamite manner. He made regular contributions to the "Anti-Jacobin Review", "The British Review", "The Electic Review" and the "Edinburgh Review". Later on, he wrote in a periodical called the "Philanthropist" with cooperation of William Allen. All his contribution mostly related with education, the freedom of the press and the prison discipline. The university of London was established in 1825. He played a significant role in founding the above university.

James Mill wrote "Liberty of the Press", "Prisons and Prison Discipline", "Colony and Education" etc. in 1814. The publication of "History of British India" brought him immediate immense fame. As a result of this he was appointed an official in the India House in 1819. He became the head of the Examiner's office in 1830. During this period he wrote the "Elements of Political Economy."

After the death of Bentham, he became the leader of the utilitarian school. James Mill exercised tremendous influence on his contemporaries. Lord Brongham, George Grote, Joseph Hume, Rocbuck and Ricardo came under his influence. Among them Ricardo was his best friend.

James Mill showed extraordinary leanings for law and law reforms. According to him neither monarchy nor aristocracy was suitable for the people. He favoured the representative government for the people. At the same time the representative must act as a check on the abuses of the legislature. He stood for frequent elections to approve or disapprove of the representatives.

James Mill was not in favour of universal suffrage. According to him the right to vote should not be given to women. He also did not believe that the right of voting should be given every man. It should be given only to those men who were of the age of 40 and above.

James Mill believed that all men pursued their own pleasure and avoided pain. To protect the rights of man authority is needed. Government provides this authority. His desire was to strengthen the House of Commons to meet the obstacle posed by the King and the House of Lords. Hence he condemned the House of Lords. He also put forth certain reforms in the House of Lords with a view to decrease its powers. He anticipated the Parliament Act of 1911 when he said that "Let it be enacted that if a bill which has been passed by the House of Commons and thrown out by the House of Lords is renewed in the House of Commons in the next session of Parliament and passed but again thrown out by the House of Lords it shall if passed a third time in the House of Commons, be law, without being again sent to the Lords."

James Mill regarded the middle class as the natural leaders of the people. This class also had the sympathy for the lower classes. It was in good position to guide and lead the people. Hence he stood for the supremacy of the middle class.

James Mill was not opposed to the king. To him the interests of the King were bound up with the interests of the people. If he acted against the interests of the people, he became a curse.

Like Bentham, James Mill stressed the need for education. All men were by nature equal and the differences among them were due mainly, to education. The end of education was to give happiness to the people as a whole. According to him, education was all powerful "If education does not perform everything, there is hardly anything which it does not perform." Here he echoed the doctrine of Helvetins that "a prodigious difference is produced by education...."

Like Bentham, Mill advocated many reforms in the field of jurisprudence and international law. According to him jurisprudence was concerned with rights and not with their creation and distribution. It belonged to the legislature. Jurisprudence is concerned with the protection and security of rights. He stood for international law and the pressure of international public opinion would compete the nations to obey international law and justice. There was a necessity of the codification of international law and the establishment of an international tribunal with a well defined procedure. He handled in a better and fitter way the subject of war and the rights and obligations of belligerants.

It cannot be denied that Mill's version of utilitarianism was illuminated with historical, economic and psychological analysis which Bentham had been unable to supply.

■ ■

XVI

John Austin (1790–1859)

Early Life : John Austin was a famous English lawyer. He is considered as the most influential English writer on Jurisprudence. He was the disciple of Bentham. Austin was born on 3rd March, 1790. At the age of sixteen, he joined the army and served as a Lieutenant in Malta and Sicily upto 1812. After resigning the job, he began to study law. He was called to the Bar in 1818. He practised the legal profession for seven years in Lincoln's Inn. But it did not suit his taste. His military experiences had a profound influence upon the development of his doctrine of sovereignty and the theory of law. In 1819, he married Sarah Taylor, a beautiful, talented, brilliant, fascinating and remarkable woman. After their marriage, Austin became neighbours in London of Bentham and the Mills.

Austin was appointed Professor of Jurisprudence in the newly founded University of London in 1826. In the following year he went to Germany along with his wife. There he was greatly influenced by the German ideas of classification and systematic analysis. In 1828, they returned home. His opening lectures in 1828 were attended by John Start Mill, George Cornwall Lewis, Romily etc. Later on he failed to attract new students and in 1832 he resigned the professorship in bitter despair and disappointment.

John Austin was appointed in 1833 to the Criminal Law Commission but he resigned that post too after signing its first two reports because of utter frustration. In 1836, hc was appointed commissioner with George Cornwall Lewis to give advice on the legal and constitutional reforms of Malta. He went back to England in 1848 and lived with his wife in Paris until his death in December 1859.

His works : Austin wrote with extreme difficulty. His best known work is "The Province of Jurisprudence Determined." It was published in 1832 in the form of six lectures. The second edition of "The Province of Jurisprudence Determined" was published by his widow Sarah Austin in 1861. She also reconstructed from the notes of her husband the main "Lectures on Jurisprudence or the Philosophy of Positive Law." She published them in 1863. The substance of his political philosophy is chiefly to be found in this work "Lectures on Jurisprudence" as edited by Cambell after the death of Mrs. Austin.

According to Lord Melborne "Province of Jurisprudence Determined" was the dullest book that he had ever read. John Bowle says that the style of Austin is generally clear, if dry and sometimes achieves a severe eloquence.

His Political Philosophy

(a) *State*: Austin did not accept the Social Contract Theory. According to him, it is artificial, unrealistic, fictitious, false and superfluous. People obeyed the state not due to any formal consent but due to force of their habit of obedience. The state continues to exist on account of its utility to the people.

(b) *Rights and duties* : Austin disfavoured natural rights. In his aspect he resembles Bentham. He held that all rights were created by law and that political restraint as necessary as civil liberty. Further he remarked that all rights were created and regulated by the state. According to him, duty was enforced by the power of the state.

(c) *Liberty*: According to Austin, the extent of the liberty of the people depended upon what sovereign was prepared to give them. He had no belief in absolute freedom. He realised and recognised that law secured liberty and that without law there can be no liberty. The sovereign was not limited by any law in its power of narrowing or widening the bounds of liberty. According to the principle of utility the sovereign may be narrowed or widened the bounds of liberty. He enforced the positive law for the good of the people. Thus, his concept of liberty was aimed at the welfare of the whole community.

According to him, international law depended only on moral sanctions. There was no hope of general obedience to a supranational law. Sovereign power was superior.

(d) *Utility* : According to him, God's intention is the promotion of the greatest happiness of all His sentiment creatures and so his command is that all his human action be directed towards the achievement of that end. Some actions of man are good, some of them are bad. Hence God prevents those bad actions which would hinder the promotion of the greatest happiness. Thus, he equates his principle utility with God's command.

(e) *Law*: According to Austin, Law is the command of the sovereign. It is issued by a person, who is politically superior to those who are politically inferior. Austin calls these commands issued by the sovereign in a state as positive laws or laws proper. Further he differentiate the positive law from law of God i.e. fundamental principle of morality and from positive morality. The science of Jurisprudence is called positive law, whereas positive morality is concerned with science of legislation morals and positive international morality. Political sovereign make those positive laws. Positive morality are set by persons who have no political authority e.g. by parents over the children. According to Austin "every positive law is let by a sovereign person or sovereign body of persons, to a member or members of the independent political society wherein that person or body of persons is sovereign or supreme." Austin developed his theory of sovereignty from this principle.

Theory of Sovereignty

John Austin was a famous English lawyer. He wrote a book on Jurisprudence entitled "Lectures on Jurisprudence". It was published in 1832. His theory is the outcome of the teachings of Bentham and Hobbes. This theory is based on the nature of law. According to Austin, "law is a command given by a superior to an inferior." In the word of Austin, "If a determinate human superior not in the habit of obedience, to a like superior receives habitual obedience from the bulk of a given society, that determinate superior sovereign in that society, and the society (including the sovereign) is a society political and independent." From this definition we can explain the same in the following manner:

(i) The sovereignty is determinate.

(ii) The sovereignty is indivisible.

(iii) The sovereignty is absolute and unlimited.

(iv) The sovereign is human, i.e. he is not super natural.

(v) The sovereign is superior, i.e. society includes a chain of inferiors and superiors and the sovereign is the last link of that chain.

(vi) The sovereign receive obedience from the bulk of the society. It means that some members of the society may disobey the laws and hence the obedience is not from the whole society.

(vii) The sovereign does not habitually obey another superior. It means that the sovereign may occasionally submit himself to laws, set by opinions or to commands of determinate parties.

Austin says that the Sovereign is a determinate person or body of persons. He is acting as the final source of power. His authority is unlimited. All citizens, unions, associations and other things are under the control of the sovereign. Directly or indirectly he is not subject to any control in the state. He is an unquestionable man. So long as the laws emanate or come out from the legal sovereign they are called commands of the Sovereign which must be obeyed. The Sovereign receives habitual obedience from the bulk of the community. The command of the Sovereigns is the essence of law. Law is in the form of "You must do certain things" or "You must not do other things". If a person fails in both the cases he would be punished.

From the above analysis of his theory, we know that the Sovereign has supreme power which is determinate, absolute, illuminable, inalienable, all comprehensive and permanent. There is no rival to him. There is no other supreme power in his territory.

Criticism : The theory of Austin has been criticised by many writers including Sir Henry Maine. He criticises the unlimited power of the sovereign as stated by Austin. From history Sir Henry Maine has given examples that there is no power on earth which can wield unlimited powers. It cannot be denied that the government is the source of power and authority in the state. But even then it cannot control the morality of the people. Further Maine says that Ranjit Singh actually controlled the people of Punjab. But he could not change the customs of the people, their religious belief and superstition. Hence it is wrong to say that

Sovereign is possessed of un-limited powers.

Prof. Laski has also attacked the theory on the similar point. He says that it is impossible to exercise unlimited powers. Further it is also undesirable to give unlimited powers to anybody. Many examples can be cited from history for this. If unlimited power is given to a king or queen in a particular country, there we cannot see the freedom of the people. They would turn as dictators and suppress the people.

In the federal form of government, there is no place for the unlimited sovereign. In U.S.A. the Congress, the states and the President are enjoying the powers. Amendment to the constitution can be made in the U.S.A. by two-thirds majority of the congress and three-fourths of the state.

It is already mentioned by Austin that sovereign is a dcterminate body. This principle of Austin has also been criticised by modern writers. For this also we can quote the U.S.A. for example. In U.S.A. there is no such determinate body having unlimited powers. There the Congress, the Governors of the states, the President and the Supreme Court have limited powers.

Again the absolute and indivisible character of Sovereignty is questioned by the pluralists. If the power of the sovereign is divided he cannot control the whole society. Hence the idea of divided sovereignty has to be accepted.

Austin says that law is essentially a command of the sovereign. Law is universal and uniform for all the people but command is not. Every one must obey the law whereas the man who gives the command himself does not obey it.

Further the pluralists like Laski challenge the supremacy of the state on the ground that state is one among the many associations found in the society and so it cannot be endowed with any superior power.

Finally, the emergence of international law backed by world opinion expressing through the U.N.O. puts definite limits to the authority of the state. From the above facts it is difficult to believe that sovereignty is absolute or unlimited.

■■

XVII
John Stuart Mill (1806–1873)

His life: John Stuart Mill is the most widely known nineteenth century British political writer. He was the last of the utilitarians and the foremost of the individualists. He was the eldest son of James Mill. He was born in London on May 20, 1806, No child of James Mill underwent a more "unusual and remarkable" boyhood than young John Stuart Mill according to R.G. Gupta. This fact has been admitted by J.S. Mill himself in his Autobiography which was written during the last five years of his life (1873).

James Mill had a very good plan to bring him up in the Benthamite lines. He was learning Greek by the age of three. At eight he began to study Latin. He studied Greek and Latin classics which included those of Plato, Herodotus, Xerophen, Thucydides, Homer and Polybias. He also learnt algebra geometry, the differential calculus etc. He studied political economy particularly Adam Smith and David Ricardo. His father was his teacher and constant companion.

At the age of 23 he left the Debating Society which he himself founded. The reason that he adduced is that "he had enough of Speech making." Before the age of 32 he had already worked as the editor of the London and Westminster Magazine." J.S. Mill was appointed to a clerical post in the East India Company in 1823 and became head of his department in 1856. He continued in that post till 1858 when the East India Company was ended and the Government of India was taken over by the Crown.

J.S. Mill's association with Mrs. Harriet Taylor, a woman of high character and brilliant mind paved the way for a great attachment towards her. He married her in 1851, two years after the death of her husband. It is doubtless true that Mrs. Taylor helped to humanise his revised version of utilitarianism. His view was that she was the originator of most of his ideas. After the ending of the company, he refused to accept an offer of a government post, preferring to retire from the administrative service. At the age of 59, he entered Parliament and sat there from 1865 to 1868. He was defeated in the elections in 1858.

After his retirement he lived along with his wife till her death in 1858. He spent most of his time in France with his step-daughter, Helen Taylor, as a companion. He died on 8th May, 1873 at Avignon where he now lies buried in a tomb with his wife.

His works: Mill's first great literary achievements were in the Westminster Review. By his pen he brought himself into prominence. He was a great writer and he wrote a large number of books, pamphlets and articles. In 1843, he published his *System of Logic* and achieved immense success. He published the *Principle of Political Economy* in 1848. It became his immediate and exceptional success. *Considerations on Representative Government*, *Utilitarianism*, *The Subjection Women* were published respectively in 1860, 1861 and 1869. His *Autobiography* was edited by his daughter Helen Taylor and published in 1873 posthumously. *The Three Essays on Religion* another posthumous work was published in 1874. Apart from this, his another most famous work *On Liberty* was published in 1859. As the editor of the *London Review*. John Mill was a regular contributor to the journal from its start in 1834 until 1840.

Green expressed his respect for him by echoing Gladstone's remark that Mill was a saintly man. He considered Mill to have been an "extraordinarily good man." The above comments are Mills' true epitaph. According to C.L. Wayper. "In the whole history of Political Philosophy, there are few more appealing characters than his."

His views: (a) *Utilitarianism* : J.S. Mill decided to modify some of the basic tenets of utilitarianism to defend the same from the anti hedonist movement led by Carlyle. He opined that some pleasures are of a higher quality than others. For Bentham and James Mill pleasures differ only in quantity. Bentham has put it as "quantity of pleasure being equal, pushpin is as good as poetry". Mill offers a singular proof that Bentham is wrong. But Mill truly reflects human experience when he says that it is better to be a human being dissatisfied than a pig satisfied; better to be Socrats dissatisfied than a fool satisfied. And if the fool or the pig is of a different opinion, it is because they only know their own side of their question. The other party to the comparison knows both sides." It is surely non-utilitarian view.

According to Mill pleasures cannot be measured in an objective manner. The specific cause is, he said absurd and men have always relied upon the testimony of those most competent to judge." According to C.L. Wayper "what means are there of determining which is the acutest of two pains or the intensest of two pleasurable sensations except the general suffrage of those who are familiar with both?" This argument clearly indicates the hollowness of utilitarianism.

Mill maintained the further non-utilitarian position by holding the view that not principle of utility but the dignity of man is the final end of life. Here J.S. Mill approved of Humboldt's doctrine of "self-realisation." He asked that what more or better can be said of any condition of human beings than that it brings human beings themselves near to the best thing they can be." This doctrine of "self-realisation" had already been attacked by Bentham and James Mill. Their main aim was the achievement of pleasure and the avoidance of pain. To him state was a moral institution with a moral ends i.e. the promotion of virtue in the individual. Utilitarians have always subordinated liberty to the principle of utility; but to Mill, Liberty is a more fundamental end than utility.

b. *Liberty*: J.S. Mill in his most famous essay "On Liberty" has given a very valuable and significant views about individualism and laissez faire. He was a powerful defender of individual liberty. There should not be any interference by the government in the affairs of the individual. Every individual was to be allowed to develop himself of his own lines. According to him, liberty is the sovereignty of the individual over himself. Interference with the individuals' liberty is justified only when it is meant to prevent him from harming others. The sum and substance of the thesis of his essay is; "The sole end for which mankind are warranted individually or collectively in interfering with the liberty of action of any of their member is self protection. The only purpose for which power can be rightfully exercised over any member of a civilised community, against his will, to prevent harm to others. His own good, either physical or moral is not a sufficient warrant. The only part of the conduct of anyone for which he is an uable to society is that which concerns others. In the part which merely concerns himself his independence is absolute. Over himself, over his own body, and mind individual is sovereign."

Mill divided all actions of the individuals into two categories viz., self-regarding actions and other regarding actions. If an individual was to be allowed to do whatever he was pleased to do as regards those actions in which he alone was concerned are self regarding actions. If his actions affected others, that actions can be called other regarding actions. In this connection it is pointed out that all that an individual so as affect others. There is nothing that affects him alone in the state.

Mill gave a classic definition for the appropriate sphere of human liberty. The inward domain of conscience, liberty of thought and expression, absolute freedom of opinion and sentiment of all subjects, scientific, moral, theological, practical or speculative are included in it. Every individual should be given freedom of taste and pursuits. Without doing any harm to others they should have the right of freedom to unite for any purpose.

Mill wanted to promote the development of individual men and women for he was satisfied that all wise and noble things come and must come from individuals. According to him, there can be no self-development without liberty. It is necessary for the happiness of society.

Further Mill defined the term 'liberty' as that "Liberty consists in doing what one desires." Again he added that "Liberty consists in doing what one desires and does not desire to fall into the river.'' Thus he emphasised the non-interference in the affairs of the individual.

c. *Democracy* : After making a thorough analysis of the defects of democracy, he came to the conclusion that it is not suitable for all people. However, the best form of government is representative government. He stood for proportional representation. The right of vote should be given to all those who were qualified to vote. He advocated the enfranchisement of women. Certain qualifications were suggested by him. Public voting and plural voting were advocated by him.

d. *His views on women*: It cannot be denied that Mill had rendered ye man service to the cause of women. He did the same not only inside of the Parliament but also outside of the Parliament. According to him sex should not be a disqualification to them. Women were denied jobs on par with men in public offices. They were thrown into the background on account of customs and prejudices. Hence he stood for speedy and needy action of emancipation. As a result womenfolk achieved tremendous rights as against men including right to vote. Women all over the world have got the right to vote and they should be grateful to J.S. Mill for his vigorous and rigorous advocacy of their cause. Mrs. Taylor was partly responsible for the same for which they should show their gratitude to her for ever.

e. *Property*: J.S. Mill advocated the institution of private property. It was necessary for the good and progress of mankind. But he opposed to the view of the communists on the point of the institution of the rich people. However, he disliked the abolition of the law of primogeniture. Later on he was attracted towards socialism.

His views on Democracy : In his ''Liberty'' and ''Representative Government'' Mill shows himself very distrustful of democracy. He is one of the greatest of English writers on democracy. After making a thorough analysis he came to the conclusion that it is not suitable for all peoples. The first element of a good government is ''the promotion of the virtue and intelligence of the people." However, the best form of government is representative government.

J.S. Mill is a democrat because he believes as did Bentham that such is the innate selfishness of men that each individual's rights and interests are best defended by himself. Hence he says that the ideal type of government has to be representative. "The passion of the majority is needed to conquer the self interest of the few" according to Mill.

J.S. Mill is a democrat because he believes as also did Bentham that freedom is the means to prosperity. Without prosperity there can be no happiness. Democracy not only makes men happier but also it makes them better.

J.S. Mill identifies two kinds of dangers to representative democracy i.e. low grade intelligence in the representative body, and of class legislation on the part of numerical majority. To remove these two evils there should be restricted suffrage. The minority should be given due representation in a real democracy. He suggests the system of proportional representation for that purpose.

According to J.S. Mill, the pure idea of democracy according to its function is the government of the whole people, by the whole people, equally represented. The right of vote should be given to all those who are qualified to vote. He advocated the enfranchise of women. He says that there should be educational qualification for voters. If there is no such educational qualification, democracy is not possible for all people. But where society is ready for democracy than he is certain that all its adult members women as well as men must participate in it. In addition to the educational qualifications, the voters should also have the property qualifications. People with property should behave in a more responsible manner than the propertyless people.

Mill puts more stress on public votings, eventhough secret ballot is universally recognised today as the best system of voting. He defends public voting on the ground that "the duty of voting like any other public duty, should be performed under the eye and criticism of the public." Secret voting is bound to encourage selfishness. It is to be noted that Bentham and James Mill were the supporters of vote by secret ballot. But J.S. Mill was differ from them on this point.

In his "Representative Government" published in 1861 J.S. Mill advocates the plurality of votes to the highly educated citizens. For that purpose, he has given certain group of persons to whom should be given more than one vote. The basis of his groups were mental, cultural and moral qualities. Mill style this system as "weighted voting".

Mill was the advocate of women's suffrage. He was closely connected with the London Committee of the Society for women's suffrage. Apart from this he did yeoman service to the cause of women. It was due to his wife Mrs. Taylor. According to him, sex should not be a disqualification for them. His intention and contention was that if differences between the sexes were due wholly and solely to external circumstances. Those differences and demarcations should be removed rigorously. Those had been created by man's long continued use of women in one definite line. The differences were bound to disappear if women were given political and social freedom. Those were the outcome of the law of force and not the law of justice. If the law of justice became supreme, the law of force should be ended ultimately they were bound to disappear.

According to Mill, women should be given equal opportunities on par with men. But during his time there was no such equal opportunities. Birth should not be a barrier or an obstacle to the advancement of a person. He stood for full and speedy emancipation of women. Then only they would be happy in the new environment. Society would benefit by the practical turn of the mental capacities and characteristic of women. The services available to society will be doubled on account of the contribution of women. Hence he advocated the right of vote to women. Ultimately he succeeded in this task. Women all over the world have got the right to vote and they should be grateful to J.S. Mill for his strong advocacy of their cause.

Mill showed a difference between true and false democracy.

According to him, "Every man to count for one; no man for more than one" is a principle of false democracy. On the contracy, true democracy will give weight and influence to all the different elements of society. It will give plural votes to capable persons as me mentioned earlier.

In 1835, De Tocqueville published the first part and in 1840 the second of his "Democracy in America." It is considered the most brilliant and penetrating study of America ever written. Mill called it "the first analyical inquiry into the influence of Democracy." It exercised a tremendous and stupendous influence upon him. For many years he maintained a cordial correspondence with him. De Tocqueville regarded democracy an inevitable and it rested with man to make it a good or an evil thing. In America, democracy safeguarded the interests of the majority and greatly developed the facilities of the people. But it resulted in general want of merit in legislative and public functionaries. It produced a tyranny of the majority which according to Mill did not "take the shape of tyrannised laws but that of a dispensing power over all laws."

The question which always revolved in the mind of J.S. Mill is, "How can I make democracy safe for the world, how can I ensure that this inevitable process will be for the good and not the evil of mankind?" The answer to the question is beautifully given by Lord Lothian as, "Democracy is not a gift to be conferred but a habit to be acquired. It cannot succeed unless it produces a race of aristocrats — and an aristocrat I would define as one who puts more into life than he takes out of it."

According to Mill, True Democracy will never allow M.Ps to be paid since thereby "the calling of a demagogue would be formally inaugurated." It will insist that representative are true representatives and not mere delegates. Englishmen were reluctant to exchange this representation of interests for representation of members. He stood for the abolition of the Reform Bill based on the old view of the constitution. It is due to the distinction between False and True Democracy of Mill. He is regarded as a democrat although by 20th century standards a reluctant democrat.

■■

XVIII
Karl Marx (1818–1883)

Early Life : Karl Marx is greatly considered as the father of socialism. He was a great German philosopher. He is the most important figure in the history of socialist thinking. He was born on May 5, 1818 in the city of Treves in Prussia. His parents were Jews. He had his education at Bonn, Berlin and Jena. He studied history, philosophy and jurisprudence. But his special subjects were Jurisprudence and Philosophy. Since, his father and other members of the few embraced Christianity and baptized as Protestants, he was also educated as a Protestant. In 1841 he got his doctorate degree at Jena university. After this he expected a chance of becoming a Professor in the University. But it was denied to him due to the dismissal of his dear friend Bauer from Bonn. He became a journalist.

In 1842 Karl Marx became the editor of the "Rheinische Zeitung" wrote in a vigorous style and with confidence. In 1843, he married Jenny Von Westphalen, daughter of a high government official. In October 1843, he went to Paris where he established close contracts with French Socialists. Already he was influenced by the philosophy of Hegel and Feurbach.

Karl Marx was influenced by the writings of Hegel. At this juncture had a fine opportunity of meeting Proudhon at Paris. In September 1844, he met Friedrich Engels. Engels became his life long companion and collaborator. In January 1845, he was expelled from Paris and went to Brussels. There he along with Engels published "The Holy Family" and "Theses on Feurbach." Thereafter he went to England in the same year to study Economics. Marx and Engels during their stay in Brussels wrote the Principles of communism which was published from London in February 1848 as "The Communist Manifesto." This book gives a clear idea of Marx's whole social philosophy. In the following year he was expelled from France by the pressure of the Prussian Government. This time he settled in England where he spent the rest of his life in the midst of poverty and persistent illness.

During his stay in England he began to write about socialism. He proved himself a prolific writer in midst of sorrows and sufferings and miseries and misfortunes. Pan brokers, family troubles, illness and deaths failed to disturb him from the composition of his great book "Das Capital" the most famous book on socialism was published in 1848. It is considered as the Bible of the socialists. His other works are "A contribution to the critique of political economy", "Value Price and Profit" and "Poverty of Philosophy". Mrs Marx died in December 1881. His most favourite darling daughter died in 1883. He died on 14th March, 1883.

Marxist Theory : The Theory of Surplus Value, the materialistic interpretation of history, the theory of Class War, views against Capitalism and the theory of value are some of the main points of the philosophy of Karl Marx.

The Principle element of Marxism is the Dialectical materialism. It is a legacy from Socrates and Plato. Hegel too over this concept from Plato. Marx followed the method of Hegel in this respect. At the same time he did not accept the whole of Hegel's philosophy.

Marx gives a beautiful sketch about class war from history. There is war between the two i.e. the rich and the poor, the haves and the have nots, the employer and the employees, the exploiter and exploited and the landlord and the tenants. Here the dialectical principle is applied to the social struggle between the bourgeoisie (thesis) and the proletariat (anti-thesis) leading to the classless society (negation of negation-synthesis). This dialectical principle is related to the ultimate breakdown of the capitalist system. He refers the French Revolution that broke out in France in 1789 between the privileged and the unprivileged. This idea was followed during the Russian Revolution in 1917.

Karl Marx gives great importance to labour. The value of a commodity depends upon the quantity or amount of labour put into produce it. The difference between the value of a commodity produced by the labourer and the wages received by him is called the surplus value by Marx. Since labour is very essential for the production of a commodity, the whole of the value of price of the thing should be given to the labourer. Practically the owner gives a small amount to the labourer and takes the rest. Thus the labourer is exploited by the owner or the capitalists.

Marx says that the economic conditions are very essential for the course of history. Man must eat to live, so the production and distribution should be regulated in a proper manner. Otherwise there will be political Revolution for social and economic changes.

Karl Marx says that one day or other the capitalism should be destroyed due to the concentration of wealth in few hands. As a result of this rich become richer and the poor become poor and poorer. In due course of time the number of poor will increase in leaps and bounds and they will destroy the Capitalists ultimately.

Regarding the theory of value Marx says that all real economic value is created by human labour alone. Hence labour is very essential to produce a commodity. In that case the other factors of production like land, capital and organisation are not essential.

Marxist theory of state is not simple and monolithic. He regards state as a class institution. It is used by the bourgeoisie for the exploitation of the proletariat. After the establishment of the proletarian dictatorship the state will be disappeared.

According to Marx religion is the opium of the people, "the criticism of religion" Marx said is the beginning of all criticism. According to Marx, "Man makes religion, religion does not make Man.... Man is the world of men the state and society. This state, the society produce religion.... It is the opium of the people. He linked religion with capitalist exploitation. It is the tool in the hands of the capitalist to deceive the masses. He condemns religion since it is a bulwark of social injustice and inequality. There is no place for religion in the philosophy of Marx which attributed everything to the economic factor.

Marx's view of religion is related to his concept of alienation. According to him human beings have been alienated from the product of their work. The buyers of the products do not think of the persons who created them. It is due to division of labour. He believed in modern technology.

Criticisms : The theory of surplus value has been criticised severely. It gives much importance to labour ignoring the other factors of production. To produce each and every commodity a man has to seek the help of some machines, electricity charges, rent etc. besides natural gifts of coal and minerals. Moreover the capitalist has to pay certain taxes, electricity charges, rent etc. In this situation it is not possible to give the whole value of the commodity to the labourer. Hence the theory of Marx regarding value is wholly wrong. This same thing will apply to the theory of value also.

The materialistic interpretation of History of Karl Marx is incorrect, because he does not give due regard to other conditions like political and religious in shaping the history. Further his approach to history is very narrow.

The idea of class war given by Marx is also incorrect. There is no such war as described by Marx in any period of history.

State is not a class institution as stated by Marx. It is for the welfare of the society. It will not disappear on any account. It will remain for ever. The views regarding religion is also baseless and meaningless.

Estimate: It goes without saying that Marx was a prophet to the communists. Because he predicted a proletarian revolution in Russia. Accordingly the revolution took place in Russia in 1917. However tho greatness of Marx cannot be denied. He gave a philosophy which changed the entire face of the world. His name is the most popular name in the world. His writings are read by millions in every nook and corner of the world. According to C.L.

Wayper "Marx succeeded because he was such an explosive compound of Hebrew prophet and scientific profounder of political and economic theory." He further adds "Through Years of bitter poverty, Marx applied himself to the task of constructing scientific socialism and the magnitude of his achievement cannot be denied by even his most unsympathetic critic." It is due to the power of his message and for the inspiration of his teaching he had to be given a highest place in the world's greatest masters of political thought.

Karl Marx on class struggle

Karl Marx was a great German philosopher. He is the most important figure in the history of socialist thinking. He is considered as the father of scientific socialism. He has given a graphic picture of the theory of class war in his famous books 'Das Capital' and 'The Communist Manifesto.'

The Marxian theory of class struggle or class war is closely connected with Materialistic Interpretation of History. It also follows from the theory of surplus value. According to Marx' society was divided into two parts viz. the rich and the poor, the exploiter and the exploited. There could no co-ordination and co-operation between the two. There was bitterness and hatred among them.

The Communist Manifesto begins, "The history of all hitherto existing society is the history of class struggle." At every stage in history there is a war between the classes. The land owner verses the landless and factory owner verses the workers. The capitalist society is called a class society. The actions of those classes are called class actions. According to Marx "Freeman and slave, patrician and plebeian, lord and serf, guild master and journey-man, in a world oppressor and the oppressed, stood in constant opposition to one another carried an uninterrupted now hidden, now open fight that each time ended either in a revolutionary reconstitution of society at large or in the common ruin of the contending classes."

If we turn the pages of history we come across almost every-where a complicated society with various orders and social rank.

In ancient Rome, there were patricians knights plebeians and slaves. In the Middle Ages there were feudal lords vassals, guildmasters, journeyman apprentices and serfs. In almost all of these classes again there were subordinate gradations. "The modern bourgeois society that has sprouted from the ruins of feudal society did not do away with class antagonism. It has established new classes, new conditions of oppress on new forms of struggle in the place of the old one." In short capitalist class confronts the proletariat. By applying dialectical method it is said that the capitalism is the thesis, the organised labour is called the anti-thesis and clash between the two is called the final synthesis the classless society will emerge.

According to Marx, the modern bourgeoisie is itself the product of a long course of development of series of revolutions in the modes of production and exchange.

The history of humanity is the history of class struggle. It is the struggle of the exploiter against the exploited. It is the struggle of the rich against the poor. It is the struggle of the underdog against his master. Whatever the form of struggle the fact of class war is fundamental.

To him, the French Revolution was a bourgeois revolution. It was a revolution of the unprivileged against the privileged class. The bourgeoisie dethroned the nobility and the clergymen from their position of power and authority and established their supremacy. Another stage of the revolution was of the Proletariat to overthrow the supremacy of the bourgeois and establish their own authority.

Karl Marx considered Augustin Thierry as "The father of class struggle in French historical writings. It cannot be denied that Karl Marx was responsible for making the idea of class war, a major factor in world politics.

Marx speaks of two forms of struggles namely, economic struggle and political struggle. The economic struggle is waged for increased wages a shorter working day and better conditions of work. The workers have to take part in political struggle against the capitalists. At the same time they have to wage war against the government that supports that class. According to Marx, the workers must have a proletarian political party. The duty of the proletarian political party is to educate the people in the ideas of socialism and to guide the mass working class movement. Both economic and political forms of struggle are not ends in themselves, they are means to the end. It is freedom from exploitation. Hence Marx says that, "The class struggle is the main spring of events."

Criticisms : Many criticisms have been levelled against the idea of class war of Marx. According to some critics, it is both bad and harmful. The idea of class war teaches hatred and ill-will instead of sympathy and goodwill. It is a battle cry which is at once "Causeless and abominable." It produced harmful and painful results in the past. For e.g. it was responsible for the wholesale massacre of the middle classes in Russia and the total confiscation of their property.

It is also pointed out that the theory of class war is false. It fails to interpret and explain the actual course of human history. If we turn the pages of history we cannot give even a single example from any period of history that there was a clear cut division between the rich and the poor. From the history it is very clear that there was intermingling and intermarriages among the various sections of people. The history of the classes has been more synthetic than analytical. Further each main class is sub-divided into mary groups. It is the task of man to bring together all those groups to act against all the groups belonging to another class. So this idea of class war is pessimistic and over dramatic.

Marxism then is an optimistic doctrine of inevitable progress and of the ultimate triumph of man. This view of Marx is also criticised by modern writers. It is not the triumph of man; it can be called as his failure in history.

Dialectical Materialism : Karl Marx was a prolific writer. In his writings he has given a beautiful sketch about the dialectical materialism. It is the principal element in Marxism. The dialectical method was originated during the time of Socrates and Plato. Hegel took over the concept of dialectist from Plato. Marx borrowel this idea of dialectic from Hegel. But he applied the same for a different purpose.

To Hegel, dialectics meant something more than compromise criticism or development by stages. It may be defined as the theory of the union of the opposites i.e. discussion and debate with a view to arrive at the truth. In other words, the derivation of truth from discussion and debate. According to Hegel every proposition has both subject and predicate. But each and every predicate proves on examination to be in complete or self-contradictory.

According to Hegel, the progress of human civilisation had been in a positive straight line. It was a zig-zag sort of movement. The world is not static. It is a dynamic world. The true concept must be an active moving process, a process of evolution. In the process of evolution, something that is undeveloped gets developed by splitting up, assuming many different and opposing forms. It then unites or combines again in a new concrete objects and becomes a unity in diversity. The higher stage in the process of evolution is the realisation of the lower. The lower form is negativated in the higher. It gets carried over or sublimated. The whole process of evolution was given the name of dialectic by Hegel.

The universe of known experience was in constant flux. It was moving towards a definite point. There was imminent necessity for the ends and purpose of that evolution. The whole process of evolution was governed by definite rational principles of *thesis*, *anti-thesis* and *synthesis*. He called in the process of being, nothing and becoming of thesis, antithesis and synthesis. He gave the famous example of the genus changing into specie as a result of the sublation of differentiated. According to him, we began with an abstract universal concept called the thesis. The concept gives rise to contradiction called anti-thesis. The contradictory concepts are reconciled in the third called synthesis. It is the union of the other two concepts.

The Theory of dialectical materialism was completed by Marx in the year 1846. Dr. Engels also gave a statement regarding this theory in 1878. It is in essence a method of searching for truth in which two persons' contradictory opinion take part.

In the dialectical method, Marx never mentioned what he meant by materialism. But he made it clear that his materialism, was dialectical and not mechanical. In mechanical materialism, evolution is the path taken by material things under the pressure of their environment. In dialectical materialism, evolution is the development of matter from within environment helping or hindering but neither originating the evolutionary process nor capable of preventing it from reaching its inevitable goal. Marx wanted to change the world i.e. wanted to change for the better world by applying this principle.

According to Karl Marx, the dialectical principle is of universal application in as much as all development is the struggle of opposites "or" conflict of opposites. Each stage reached in the march to the classless society, the thesis, calls into being its opposite or anti-thesis, and from the clash between the two a new synthesis emerges. The same process would continue till the perfect goal has been achieved. Marx defines dialectics as the science of the general laws of motion both of the external world and of human thought. Thus Marx believes in historical materialism on the one hand and dialectical materialism on the other.

From the above facts it is quite clear that Marx had followed very closely the ideas of Hegel. According to C.L. Wayper, "For Hegel the universal substance was spirit. For Marx it was Matter. Both Spirit and Matter need to develop themselves and both do so by means of an inner dialectic. For Hegel the inevitable goal was the idea fully conscious of itself; for Marx the goal was the classless society perfectly organised for production sufficient for itself. In this connection, Lenin had beautifully remarked that it is very difficult to understand Marx without reading Hegel.

In the Communist Manifesto, the necessity for the dialectical process is argued in a vivid manner. In it Marx shows that human societies have developed dialectically because for the interaction between the continually changing methods by which men have performed the most essential business of their lives. It is seen from the dialectics that no system is permanent. As a result every historically developed social form is in fluid movement. To put it in a nutshell the dialectical principle viz. thesis, anti-thesis, synthesis is applied to social struggle between the bourgeoisie (thesis), the proletariat (anti-thesis) leading to the classless society (negation of negation synthesis). In this way, the principle of dialectism is related to the ultimate breakdown of the capitalist system.

According to Marx, all history is a history of class conflict. The conflict and confrontation between the bourgeoisie and the proletariat is relentless and in this struggle, the dialectical principle shows that bourgeois will go under and the exploiters shall be exploited. Consequently, the entire structure of society will be transformed.

According to Marx, two contradictions faced each other in society. Capital was the thesis and labour was its anti-thesis. Under the circumstance what was the synthesis? According to Marx, capital had completed its cycle of evolution. It was dissolving. In the circumstances stated above capital had developed the technique of large scale production to perfection. It had fulfilled an important function of transforming individual labour process into "a combined social labour process." It paved the way for the increase of capital and the increase of workers. Now arose the conflict between the exploiter and the exploited. For production and protection they had to co-operate with each other. Thereby, they decided to achieve restricted hours of work, uniform wage and uniform working days. In the evolution of society social control followed closely upon the heels of capitalism.

According to Sabine "the history of human civilisation is a succession of national cultures in which each nation brings its particular and timely contribution to the whole human achievement." As Marx wrote in the preface to the second edition of Das Capital, "In Hegel's writings dialectic stands on its head. You must turn it right way up again, if you want to discover the rational Kernel that is hidden away within the wrappings of mystification."

It has been pointed out that an evolutionary philosophy, dialectical materialism has much to commend itself. However, as a revolutionary philosophy explaining social cause and effect it has been much to condemn itself.

■■

XIX

Friedrich Engels (1820–1895)

Early life : Friedrich Engels was born on September 28, 1820 at Rhineland, the industrial town of Bermen. His father was a wealthy and prosperous cotton manufacturer. His father was a stern protestant. Hence he had no sympathy with the radical views of his son. At the age of 17 he was employed as a manager in one of his families cotton mills. Then he was sent to Manchester as the agent of his Father's business. When he was in England he got first hand knowledge of social conditions of that country. The pitiable plight of the slum dwellers in England created a deep impression in his mind. Hence his mind rapidly drifted towards the tenets of revolutionary socialism.

His works: As Engels was acquainted with the social conditions in England, he gained for himself a European reputation by his work, "The condition of the working classes in England" which was published in 1844. In this book, he criticised capitalism. In 1844, Marx and Engels associated in the formation of the groups of working class radicals. The meeting of their groups i.e. the Congress was held in 1847 in London. It was called the Communist League. In 1848, both of them jointly produced the famous "Communist Manifesto."

In 1848, both Engels and Marx took an active part in the revolutionary activities in France and Germany. After the failure of the movement, they went to England. Dr. Engels began to look after the business of his father once again. He helped his friend Karl Marx in solving his financial difficulties. In 1869, he retired from business and gave all his time to political activity and writing.

Dr. Engels collaborated with Marx on several of his works.

He himself wrote separately "Socialism Utopian and Scientific" "Anti-Duhring", "The Origin of the Family", "Private Property"and "the State". After the death of Karl Marx, Engels edited the second and third volumes of the Das Capital. He died on 5th August, 1895.

The partnership between Karl Marx and Friedrich Engels is considered as the most famous partnership in history. The quick mind and ready understanding of Engels attracted Karl Marx greatly. It led to Marx to write about him in the following manner: "You know that I am slow to grasp things and that I will always in your foot prints." But Dr. Engels never hesitated to co-operate with Marx. He played "second fiddle" to Marx's exceptional genius, Thus he remained as the most faithful and favourite disciple of Marx.

Estimate: Dr. Engels had a great sense of fun. It is pointed out that he was more worldly than Marx. He was a tall man; he had a military bearing. No doubt he was a good linguist. His favourite thing was fox hunting. He had a relish for beer especially if it was the Viennese.

Berlin in his "Karl Marx — His life and Environment" says that "Engels was a man of solid and robust, but hardly creative mind; a man of exceptional integrity and strength of character of many varied gifts, but in particular endowed with a remarkable capacity for the rapid assimilation of knowledge. He possessed a shrewd and lucid intellect and a firm sense of reality which few if any, among his radical contemporaries could claim..."

Lightheim George says that "There is a certain ambiguity about the customary interpretation of Engels share in the development of Marxism. For the Orthodox, he is simply Marx's life long ally and helper in shaping the theory and practice of the movement." He was really something more than that. Dr. Engels may be called as the father of Social Democratic Marxism. He was highly responsible in making socialism most scientific in a comprehensive way. His theoretical thinking is found in his Anti-Duhring. The formulation of scientific socialism is found in the book. It is the source of almost all the theoretical thinking of the fast growing membership of the Social Democratic Movement. If Marx was the theorist of the new proletarian movement, Engels was the propagandist and grand organiser. It is highly difficult to say which of them played the greater part. He was chiefly instrumental after the death of Marx, in giving shape to what became known as ''Orthodox Marxism''.

John Bowle says that both Marx and Engles were men of formidable ability. Both jointly created a social philosophy of massive range and insight. The authority of science was invoked by them for political beliefs. They were actuated by a burning sense of mission. Apart from this they were convinced that they would succeed only when the masses were behind them. In spite of all this, history has chosen to give Marx the greater credit ascribing to Engles, the role of a junior partner.

■■

XX

Herbert Spencer (1820–1903)

His life: Herbert Spencer was the most ardent advocate of individualism during the 19th century. He was born in 1820 in Derby in England. He was the son of a teacher. He got very little formal education. He was a self-educated man. He was a precocious child. He was encouraged by his father in his interest in science and technology. At the age of 17, he was a trained engineer. But he did not continue in the job for long. Then he showed his interest towards political economy, sociology, biology and philosophy. He became the sub-editor of a journal called "The Pilot" at the age of 24. He served as a sub-editor of "The Economist" from 1848 to 1853. Later on, he became a free writer.

His works: At the age of 30, he published his famous book called "Social Statics" in 1851. His other publications are "The Proper Sphere of Government", "Theory of population", "Art of Education", "Education", "The Social Organism", "Specialised Administration Principles of Psychology", "Descriptive Sociology, "Principles of Sociology", "Sins of Legislaters", "Synthetic Philosophy", "Justice", "Principles of Ethics", "Man verses the State", "Essays", and "Auto-biography".

It goes without saying that the writings of Herbert Spencer were translated in many languages of the world. He became famous not only in Europe and America but also in China and Japan. He was one of the few philosophers whose fame spread beyond his country in his own life time.

Theory of Evolution : Spencer introduced the concept of evolution into his political and social philosophy. The scientists of the 19th century discarded their belief in God. They put forward the idea of a life force. That force was not static but dynamic Spencer accepted the idea of perpetual evolution and applied the same to his political philosophy with a view to give more freedom of action for the individual.

Spencer held that the same basic law and evolution could be found in the physical, animal and human worlds where "transformation of the homogeneous into the heterogeneous is found there is progress".

Herbert spencer accepted the utilitarian view that happiness was the end of life. But he also added that the end was willed by the life force. To obtain happiness, he constantly adjusted himself to his surroundings. The above kind of adjustment required a certain freedom in man. It was described by Spencer as free energy and faculty. In the universe every man must be free. But his freedom should be regulated by a law of nature. Moral effort was needed by man to obey. Here he identified morality with physical laws. He reduced it to a system of automatic reactions.

According to Spencer, adjustments between several freedoms did not take place automatically in society. Men were always in the progress of adjustment. At this juncture struggle was inevitable. Hence government was very needful to help the adjustments. It should remove the obstacles of man for his free development. In the final stage there will be no necessity of state. The individuals themselves would adjust freely. Gradually, the government would be losing its control. Again it would lessen its supervision gradually. Finally anarchy was to be the destiny of Society.

Spencer applied the concepts of biology to social sciences. He pleaded for the "survival of the fittest". Evil is the result of the "non adaptation of constitution to conditions." A stern discipline was seen by him in nature. Suppose if an aged and weak animal falls prey to another beast, its death creates three kinds of happiness.

(i) The old animal is spared the suffering of slow and painful starvation.

(ii) The young ones get rid of the burden.

(iii) The beasts of prey derive happiness by killing the inferior animals.

Herbert spencer thus emphasised the stern discipline in the society.

According to Spencer, none should interfere with suffering for sentimental reasons, for such interference prevents the operation of social laws. Unfits are to be eliminated from the society since at excreted them. As a result the whole society benefits. Spencer coined the phrase "Survival of the fittest", which was later followed by Charles Darwin to explain that stage which ensured the improvement of the quality of the human race.

Spencer expressed himself against the poor laws. He opined the state as an organism like a human being. He interpreted the state in terms of biology. The attributes of an organism and the state are similar.

(i) Both of them begin as germs, simplc in structure. As they grow and develop, they become complex.

(ii) In both the organism and the society there is mutual dependence of parts.

(iii) Both of them are subject to wear and tear and there is replacement in both of them.

(iv) Both have a sustaining, distributory and regulating system.

In explaining the structure of the both he said "As the lowest type of animal is all stomach respiratory surface or limb, so primitive society is all warrior, all hunter, all builder or all tool maker. As society grows in complexity division of labour follows i.e. new organs with different functions in the animals in which fundamental trait, they become entirely alike."

Further according to him, the sustaining system of an organism is its digestive system; the sustaining system of society is its productive system including industries and agriculture. The distributory system of an organism is the circulatory system means of communication and transport serve as the distributory system of the society; the nervous system is the regulating system in an organism; the government is the regulating system in the society.

(i) In spite of these resemblances, Spencer pointed out certain differences between animal organism and body politic. The former was concrete in structure and its units were bound together in close contact; the latter was discrete and its units were free and more or less widely dispersed''.

(ii) In the case of animal organism, consciousness was concentrated in a small part of the aggregate; there was no ''sensorium'' in the social body.

From the above facts it is very clear that the state is an organ of society. Its sphere of activity therefore must be limited to the performance of its essential functions. These functions are the maintenance of peace and order and giving protection to its citizens. Government is an evil; it is a necessary evil. The scope of the government would diminish as civilisation develops. As and when the human the faculty's develop they became fit for social life. At that stage government will disappear. Thus he applied the biologic analogy to uphold individualism.

Spencer explained that the modern industrial state has evolved from the military state. The latter was a primitive one. It paved the way for war. The military chief became the political leader. It expanded into an industrial state and society. The life of the state was based on voluntary co-operation. The individual is regarded as the chief end of the state. Hence, it must assure maximum liberty and happiness of its members. In this form of state people are anti-militarist, anti-imperialist, cosmopolitan and humanitarian. Finally, he contented that modern industrialism would make men co-operate on a peaceful voluntary and non exploiting basis. When they reach the stage, there is no necessity for government for them. It will eventually disappear or wither away.

Individualism : Herbert Spencer was a great advocate of individualism. His first major publication was ''The Proper Sphere of Government.'' It was published in 1842. In this essay, Spencer expresses his political philosophy of extreme individualism and laissez faire. His individualism was the outcome of his belief in natural rights, natural economic laws and non-conformist's hostility to authority. Natural laws demanded that the government should allow nature to function freely without any artificial hindrance.

Spencer applied the law of organic evolution through natural selection to human society. After that he came to the conclusion that the state should allow nature to do its work. The first and foremost function of the state is to give maximum assistance to nature i.e. it is the duty of the state to allow every individual to fight out the struggle for existence according to his conduct and nature. There are two kinds of duties to the state. Firstly, the primary function of the state is defence against external danger. Secondly, it is the duty of the state to prevent encroachments reciprocally among the individuals within the state. In other words, it is described by him in these words, "Every man is free to do that which he wills provided the infringes not upon the equal freedom of any other man."

Spencer eternally opposed to all organised charity, public as well as private. He also disliked all state help to education or industry. According to him, there will not be any useful purpose by giving compulsory education to the people in the state. Moreover poor relief and social legislation seemed to serve no fruitful purpose to them in the state. The State should have no business to assist the lame, the dumb, the poor, the old and the destitute. Apart from this the state should not undertake the construction of post offices and erecting of light houses. The above functions did not come under the category of justice which alone is the function of the State.

According to Spencer, the state is not an eternal institution. Its existence was merely incidental. In his "Social Statics" published in 1866, he maintained that the individual had the right to ignore the state. In short the only right of the individual is equal freedom with everybody else. The only duty of the state is to protect that right against violence and fraud.

Spencer's philosophy of *Laissez faire* was fully expressed in his book "The Man versus the State." In it he reiterated that it was harmful and horrible to interfere with the process of the survival of the fittest. Such an interference with natural selection would lower the standards of a society as a whole.

Spencer was not in favour of socialisation of the means of production. For him "all socialism is slavery." Under Socialism or Communism, the individual would be a slave of the whole community. To him the divine right of parliaments, was a great political superstition just as the divine right of kings. He attacked the sovereignty of Hobbes.

In his essay entitled "The sins of the Legislators" he condemned the legislation passed and enforced in the past. The laws of the state were a record of "unhappy guesses". Later on some of them were repealed or amended. Thus Spencer has given a vivid account about his individualistic philosophy.

Rights : "Rights are nothing but artificial divisions of the general claim to exercise the faculties" according to Spencer. There are two kinds of rights viz. private rights and public rights. Rights concerned with the property and family of the individual are private rights. Public rights are concerned with his relations to the State. Regarding private rights he had no belief on private property. He attacked "The subjection of women". He favoured the right of vote to women. Regarding Public rights he said that government was a vicious and immoral institution. Every individual had the "right to ignore the state." In human life each individual must receive justice and he should enjoy freedom in his life. Freedom according to him is that every man should enjoy his natural rights.

Estimate : Spencer was the most ardent advocate of individualism during the 19th century. According to Maxey "No reputable political thinker of the present time acknowledge Spencer as his master. For the critical mind of today he is a amateur scientist and the pseudo philosopher. Science has learned a lot about evolution since Spencer's day. Undoubtedly, Spencer had done more to the development of biology and science after Charles Darwin.

Spencer's differentiation between the military and industrial state is of lasting influence. As Ebenstein points out in the second half of the twentieth century Spencer's basic distinction throws a great deal of light on the political behaviour of states.

Spencer had great influence in the U.S.A. like Locke, Spencer's idea on individualism applealed to the American businessmen and industrial entrepreneurs. Due to its inherent weekness Spencerism last its vigour. In cannot be denied that his law played a significant role during his life time. However his thought has not been abandoned fully.

■■

XXI

Thomas Hill Green (1836–1882)

Thomas Hill Green was an English historian and philosopher. He was also a theorist and a reformer. He was born in the year 1836 at Yorkshire. He was the son of a clergyman. He was educated at Rugby and the Balliod College, Oxford. He became professor of moral philosophy in 1878 at Oxford.

He was not only a philosopher, but was thoroughly interested in the practical politics of his country. He was elected to the Oxford Town Council by the people. For some years he served on the governing body of a system of schools in Birmingham. According to him, the basis of sound government was the local government of the country.

T.H. Green's many lectures were published after his death in 1882. In 1879 he delivered his first lecture "Lectures on the Principles of Political", "Obligation." His other publications are "Progegomena to Ethics", "Lectures on liberal Legislation", "Freedom of Contract" and "Lectures on the English Revolution."

Green's philosophy is taken from the writings of Plato, Aristotle, Rousseau, Kant and Hegel. Green agreed with the view of Aristotle that the supreme function of the state was to make it possible to realise their common good. Green borrowed from Rousseau the idea of moral freedom of man. In the purely metaphysical field Green was closer to Hegel. But in ethics and politics Kantian influence seems to be greater. He was Kantian in outlook.

According to Green, the State is the product of human consciousness. Human consciousness postulates liberty. Liberty involves rights and rights demand the State. It was an ethical institution which was essential for the moral development of man. The important function of the state was to enforce rights. The State might use its force since it expressed the general will of the people. To him "will not force is the basis of the State."

From Green's Lectures on the Principles of Political Obligation" it is seen that the people obey the State because it contributes or can contribute towards their moral life. According to him "the function of the government is to maintain conditions of life in which morality shall be possible and morality consists in the disinterested performance of self-imposed duties." The state was neither absolute nor omnipotent. It was limited both from within and from without. He believed in the "Universal Brotherhood of man." The right of every individual to life involved a check on the authority of the state.

As an active liberal in politics, Green unlike Kant and Hegel supported a representative form of government. According to Green the right to free life is the essence of citizenship. But it is subject to restriction by the state which has to use force in order to repel a force opposed to freedom. According to him the object of punishment is neither to inflict pain on the criminal in proportion to his moral guilt for it is rather impossible to assess this proportion nor to bring about a moral reformation of the criminal for all true reform comes from within.

Green viewed that right to resistance was possibly justificable and not obligatory. He rejected the meaning given to the term "Natural Law" by writers like Hobbes and Locke. He also rejected the idea of the State of nature as advocated by the writers of the social contract theory.

According to Green, State was a society of societies. The rights exercised by the State over the different societies was one of adjustment. The state adjusted for each system of rights internally. It also adjusted the system of rights to the rest externally.

The part and parcel of his theory of State action was the problem of punishment. The will of the criminal was anti-social. It was a force opposed to freedom. Punishment was a force directed against the force of the criminal. The primary object of punishment is not to reform the criminal but to create terror in his mind. The future prevention of crime is the chief object of punishment. Punishment should create a terror which will prevent others from committing the crime.

Regarding property he held liberal views. He was neither a protector of private property nor as out and out critic of it. Again it is stated that he was neither a socialist nor an individualist. Every individual must have the opportunity to acquire property because everyone has the capacity to partake of common social good. That capacity is different from man to man. As a result there was inequality in the possession of property. If a few property owner interfere in the affairs of others, it was the duty of the state to interfere. He stood for a class of small proprietors filling their own land.

There is a difference of opinion between Green and Hegel in respect of the attitude towards war. According to him war was never absolutely right. It was a cruel necessity. It was a moral wrong, whoever may be the wrong doer, destruction of life in war is a wrong. Green refused to accept the view that wars were inevitable. Wars did not exist because states existed. Wars existed because states did not fulfil their duty of maintaining the general rights.

Green was an individualist. State was the embodiment of the Divine Spirit. He never regarded the State as an end in itself. It was a means to end and that end was the full moral development of the individuals living within the State. It is the duty of the State to do everything for the free development of moral personality; but it should not do those things which are against such development. He described the General Will as "the common consciousness of a common good." He differed from Hegel in his idea of freedom.

Many criticisms have been levelled against the theory of Green. His theory of sovereignty is not satisfactory since it is based on General Will. Further he failed to note the sub-conscious factors that influence the actions of men in the states. Again in his theory of punishment he appears to forget totally the emotions of the people. His economic ideas regarding property is unsatisfactory since it leads to danger. Barker says that Green was both a soaring idealist and a sober realist." Thus the ideas of Green have been criticised by many modern writers.

Theory of States : Thomas Hill Green was an English historian and philosopher. He was also a theorist and a reformer. Sources of Green's philosophy are to be found in Plato, Aristotle, Rousseau, Kant and Hegel. Green agreed with the view of Aristotle that the supreme function of the state was to make it possible to realise their common good. Green borrowed from Rousseau the idea of moral freedom of man. In the purely metaphysical field Green was closer to Hegel. But in ethics and politics Kantian influence seems to be greater. He was Kantian in outlook.

Green was the first man in the 19th century to construct a comprehensive philosophy of state. There is a direct affinity between his metaphysics and politics between his ethics serves as a necessary in terlude.

According to Green the State is the product of human consciousness. Human consciousness postulates liberty. Liberty involves rights and rights demand the state. C.L.. Wayper points out that for all his belief that the state was the embodiment of the Divine Spirit, he never regarded the state as an end in itself. It was a means to an end and that end was the full moral development of the individuals who compose it." His ethics made him to believe passionately with Kant that everyman has a worth and dignity which forbids his exploitation for any purpose whatever. According to Green the life of the nation has no real existence except as the life of the individual composing it." It was the duty of the state to release men so that they may be able to fulfil their personalities." The functions of the state was a negative one. According to him the state cannot teach morality to men, nor can it make men moral since morality consists in "the disinterested performance of self imposed duties." It is to remove obstacles which prevent man becoming moral. The state may have to use force to control the outward acts of men, whose ultimate freedom was the end to be aimed at. According to Barker, "Green uses force to create freedom."

It is pointed out that the extent of state interference was very great. The state was constantly to adjust one group with another group. The duty of the State was to regulate the rights of its citizens. It was the duty of the State to provide compulsory education for the people. Parents could be forced to abide by the state.

To Green, the State was both natural and necessary. The state was an ethical institution. It was very essential for the moral development of man. The first and foremost function of the State was to enforce rights. If necessary it could be done through compulsion. The State was justified in using force because it expressed the general will of the people.

Green in his ''Principles of Political Obligation'' has allotted a chapter for General will. According to him will not force is the basis of the State. He believed in the existence of the General will. The real basis of the state was the General will according to him. So far as legal sovereignty is concerned he agreed with the view of John Austin. Accordingly legal sovereignty must reside in the supreme authority within the state. There is no power above itself. But behind this legal sovereign is the General will. This General will determines the habitual obedience of the people. From this we know that the General will meant the will for the state not the will of the state.

Although Green held that will not force was the true basis of the state he was fully aware that there were States in which force was predominant. He did not have any faith in those states since they could not fulfil their ideal function. Green also differed from Hegel in his conception of freedom. In the opinion of Hegel freedom is the voluntary identification of self with the laws of the state. For Green freedom is the right of a man to make the best of himself.

According to Green people obey the state because it contributes or can contribute towards their moral life. The State was neither absolute nor omnipotent. It was limited from both within and without. The law could control the external actions of the individuals and not the eternal motives. Thus from within the

State was limited. As a result the state was not able to promote the good life of the people indirectly. It could make its contribution by eliminating the obstacles in the way of the development of the personalities of the individuals. In some cases it is obviously seen that the individual was also given the right and duty of resisting the authority of the State. Further Green's view was that as the state had the power of adjustment over other groups it possessed the ultimate authority.

According to Green, State was a society of societies. He advocated international court of law. He believed in "the Universal Brotherhood of man." The right of every individual to life involved a check on the authority of the state. He was opposed to a paternal form of government. As an active liberal in politics Green unlike Kant and Hegel supported a representative form of Government and advocated the extension of franchise. Green's concept of liberty is closely connected to the Kantian concept of moral will and freedom. According to Kant, "A person who is really free is one who is morally free." The State should promote morality.

Green's treatment of the problem of punishment was the part and parcel of his theory of state action. The will of the criminal was anti-social. It constituted a force opposed to freedom. Punishment was a force directed against the will of the criminal. It was not possible for the State to measure the pain of punishment. Even if it was possible, the task of the judges will become very difficult. They will be required to give a different punishment in every case. At the same time it will not be possible to have common rules of punishment as they exist today.

The foremost aim of giving punishment is not to reform the criminal. It is neither to inflict pain on the criminal or in proportion to his moral guilt for it is rather impossible to assess this proportion nor to bring about a moral reformation of the criminal for all true reforms comes from within. The future prevention of crime is the chief object of punishment. Punishment should create a terror which will prevent other from committing the crime. The state looks not to virtue and vice but to rights and wrongs not however in order to avenge it, but in order to the consideration of the sort of terror which needs to be associated with such wrong doing in order to the future maintenance of rights." Thus he has clearly indicated above the primary object of punishment.

Green viewed that punishment was a force used as preventive to force, opposed to freedom. Punishment had a moral purpose and a positive quality. To secure freedom of action was its ultimate aim hence it was called moral. That freedom of action was for the free will of every member of the community.

According to Green, punishment had both direct and indirect effects or consequences. As regards direct effect or consequence, it was a force preventive of a force opposed to rights. So far as indirect effect is concerned punishments was and must be a reformation of the will.

View on Rights and Liberty : Thomas Hill Green was an English historian and philosopher. He was also a theorist and a reformer. Sources of philosophy are to be found in Plato, Aristotle, Rousseau, Kant and Hegel. The purpose of Green's 'Lectures on the Principles of Political Obligation' is to consider the moral function or object served by law or by the system of rights and obligations which the state enforces and in so doing to discover the ground or justification for obedience to law.

According to Green, a right is the claim of an individual to will his own ideal objects. The right arises from the self consciousness of an individual. Rights are inherent in an individual living in society. There are ideal rights in a society. It is organised on the basis of good will. To him rights should be regulated by mutual recognition. Rights are essentially a social product hence they cannot be attributed to isolated individuals. He criticised Locke's idea of natural rights. "Natural Right as right in a State of Nature which is not a State or society is a contradiction. There can be no right without a consciousness of common interest on the part of members of a society. Without this there might be certain powers on the part of individuals but no recognition of these powers by others as powers of which they allow the exercise, nor any claim to such recognition and without this recognition or claim to recognition there can be no right."

Rights can be called natural rights if we regard them as rights inherent in the moral nature of man living in society. Ideal rights are broader and deeper than actual or legal rights which are recognised at any time by a state. Rights are related to morality in the sense that they are the conditions for the attainment of the moral end recognition is given to them by the moral consciousness of individuals.

According to Green, rights are distinct from law because actual rights embodied in the laws of a country do not come up to the level of the ideal system. Rights are distinct from morality because while they can be enforced by external sanctions, morality cannot be so enforced. Right of resistance can be given to the people. He criticises the term "Natural Law". He brings clearly the difference between natural law and positive law. He denounces the idea of state of nature advocated by the writers of social contract theory. At the same time Green has interchanged the term "natural law" with the phrase "the law of God". Natural law is very useful and also responsible for the society to reach its goal. It is different from positive law and moral duty. Morality is a condition of the inner mind and its primary characteristic is freedom. Morality can never be enforced by external pressure.

According to him it is wrong to think that the state is sustained by the coercive power. On the other hand it is sustained by the General will. According to Lancaster, "A true State is one in which power is exercised according to law and for the maintenance of rights. Thus the basis of state is the evolution in the ideals and rights which are natural to man in society. Green while stating his theory of General will, rejected the theories of political obligation expounded Spinoza, Hobbes, Locke and Rousseau as being too abstract and illogical.

In his 'Lectures on Political Obligations' Green begins by analysing man's relation to nature. According to him, the most conclusive fact differentiating man from other living things is self consciousness. "Human consciousness postulates liberty. Liberty involves rights and rights demand the state." To attain an eternal or common consciousness of a common end freedom is essential for them. Thus the state itself becomes the product of this consciousness to promote the good of all.

The concept of liberty advocated by Green is closely connected to the Kantian idea of moral will and freedom. According to Kant, "A person who is really free is one morally free." The State should not check its self determination but must promote those conditions under which morality can be possible. The morality which consists in the disinterested performance of self-imposed duty. Moreover it is the duty of the State to remove all hindrances that prevent the realisation of moral will. He does not accept the view of Hegel that the State is the realisation of freedom. Man needs positive freedom. That positive freedom is for social good. It implies both legal and actual possibility.

Green discusses the question why people obey the State. People obey the State because it contributes or can contribute their moral life. State was a society of Societies. There State supremacy over the associations is limited. According to Green, the right to free life is the essence of citizenship. Rights are possessed by individuals from the state and enjoyed by them as citizens of the state. As the state is the source of those adjustments it must possess the ultimate power. To him the object of punishment is to create terror which will prevent others from committing the crime. Thus Green with his practical knowledge of the problems of the State and his faith in political liberalism tried to make individualism moral and social and idealism civilised and safe. Indeed his unshakable faith in man as a self-conscious and self moralising entity has a sound metaphysical basis.

XXII
Francis Herbert Bradley (1846–1924)

Early life: Francis Herbert Bradley was born in 1846 at Glasbury in South Wales. He was the son of the Dean of Westminster. He studied in the University college, Oxford. In 1870, he was awarded a fellowship at Merton College there. He devoted his full time in writing after his studies.

His works : Bradley's philosophy is to be found in his book called "Ethical Studies". It was published in 1876. It was his first major work. This book contained a large number of extracts from Hegel. Further he exposed the confusions of the doctrine of utilitarianism as held by J.S. Mill. His other works are "The Principles of Logic" and "My Station and its Duties." Shortly before his death, at Oxford in 1924, he was awarded the Order of Merit. He was the first philosopher to receive this honour in spite of the opposition of Lloyd George, the Prime Minister of England and King George V.

His views: Bradley's major work is very critical and constructive. He thought that it was his bounden duty to free English thought from the dominance of individualism and empiricism. His criticism rests on the Hegelian theory that nothing is completely real except the absolute and that the common sense, beliefs, scientific theories, religious dogmas and moral principles although justifiable within limits, do not contain any thing wholly true. It is pointed out that if T.H. Green was more Kantian than Hegelian Bradley was more Hegelian than Kantian.

Bradley expounds his theory of the State in his major work "My Station and its Duties." He gives a definition and a doctrine of state which is more Hegelian than that of Green. In other words he out and out follows the footsteps of Hegel. He conceives of the society as well as the state as a moral organism. An individual is an integral, organic member of this moral organism and a man is what he is because of his being a member of that moral organism.

According to Bradley, To be moral is to live in accordance with the moral tradition of one's country. It is the duty of every individual to perform those duties which his station in life expects him to perform. If he does so he obeys the law of his being. Man is a social being and it is out of the question for any individual to live alone. Since a man is a member of a community the latter exerts its influence on him from every directions. The very atmosphere which he breathes is social so that the conduct of his being implies in its very fibre relations of community, on whose welfare depends the welfare of the individual. In other words the family, the national and the civilised characters come to a child because of community. One is born as a member of a community which exerts its influence upon him at every stage. Thus the individual's consciousness of himself is inseparable from his knowing himself as a member of the community.

According to Bradley, an individual is a moral being. He is having definite social relationship in the society. At the same time he is a member of that society. These relationships represent his station in society. It is already mentioned that he is an organic member of society. Hence he must find his moral development in the context of these relationship or his station in society. Morality and moral development of a man gradually grow on the basis of his duties done by him.

To Bradley, the state is a system of wholes. It includes all communities which affect man. It is a systematic whole, informed by a common purpose or function. As such it has an outside a body of institutions; it has also an inner side a soul or spirit which sustains that body." Each and every part of this organism has a spirit and consciousness of its own. The parts are part and parcel of the organism. They know their position in the organism. Here Bradley agrees with Hegel in viewing the state as a "self-knowing and self-actualising individual." The right of regulation and control of individuals and associations are given to such states by Bradley.

Like Hegel Bradley conceives of the various social groups as being co-ordinated in and subordinated to the state. It is hence considered as one of the most important ideas of Bradley regarding the state.

Bradley admitted that no state in actual practice was a perfect embodiment of his ideal. The morality of the state was always on a lower state than the conscience of the people or ideal morality. Further an individual may seek to transcend the function allotted to his station in a particular community and may conceive of a higher organism than that of the State. This may lead to the realisation of all humanity as a divine organic whole."

In his both works "Ethical Studies" and "The Principles of Logic" he acknowledged his debt to German writers. Further he disclaimed originality. But he was never the simple "Hegelian" that some critics took him to be. In his essay on "My station and its Duties" he expresses this exposition of the Hegelian conception of social ethics. But Bradley did not hesitate to point out the drawbacks of this doctrine if taken as a complete account of the moral life. In "The Principles of Logic" he does not accept formalism; he tried to treat logic as a special science distinct from psychology on the one hand and from metaphysics on the other.

The philosophy of Bradley has been severely criticised on many grounds. Firstly, it is said that he had failed to make a dintinction between a state and society. There is a danger that this may lead to unlimited state regulation of life. It can not be denied that such a view gives too much of power into the hands of the state. Secondly, the phrase "my station and its duties" as it occurs in "Ethical Studies" is difficult to interpret. It means that one should be satisfied with whatever falls to his lot. He has no business to grumble. His only duty is to carry out the duties of his station without complaining. However such a view is not only conservative but also reactionary. It is detrimental to the growth of humanity. Thirdly, he has been called a wicked man, because there was nothing original or great in his philosophy. Most of his ideas have been found in the philosophy of Greeks. Thus the philosophy of Bradley has been criticised on many grounds.

XXIII
Bernard Bosanquet (1848–1923)

Early life : Bernard Bosanquet was an English philosopher. He was a great thinker and writer. He was born in the year 1848. During this time of his birth Europe was rocked by revolutions of France. He was the youngest son of a well to-do clergyman of Northumberland in England. He was educated at Sherburn, Yorkshire and at Harrow. While at Oxford he came under the influence of Green and Jowelt. Bosanquet spent ten years as a fellow at the University college, Oxford. In 1881, he went to London. Later on he held the Chair of Moral Philosophy at St. Andrews University of Scotland. He devoted most of his time in independent study. He was very interested in reading novels. Hence he gave many illustrations from the novels to explain his points. He died in London in 1923.

His works : Bosanquet was a prominent writer. He wrote many books. His important works are "Philosophical Theory of the State". "Social and International Ideals", "Logic", "History of Aesthetic", "The Value and Destiny of the individual" and "Knowledge and Reality."

His views: Professor Hobhouse describes Dr. Bosanquet as the most modern and most faithful exponent of Hegel. As an idealist he adopts. T.H. Green's principles but drops some of the limitations imposed on the state by Green and thus comes very near the Hegelian conception of the State. In other words, Bosanquet begins his philosophy with Rousseau and Green and ends almost in Hegel. Bosanquet was an idealist that too an Absolute Idealist. Like that of Bradley Bosanquet was led to formulate his own theory of aesthetics and of statecraft in his works.

Will : Like all idealists, Bosanquet also believed in idealism. The starting point of the theory of Bosanquet was a conception of a free moral will as advocated by Rousseau. According to him, true freedom lay in willing rational and universal objects. There are three stages in his doctrine of will viz., distinction between the *actual* will of the individual and his *real* will, distinction between the *real* will of the individual and the *general* will of society, and the state as the supreme *expression of the general will*.

(i) Bosanquet used the terms actual and real will in a technical sense. He used the term actual to describe the irrational impulsive and recalcitrant will of man. Bradley pointed out that a man exerted his actual will when be acted from moment to moments as a conscious individual. As that will was corrected and amended by what he wanted at all other moments and was adjusted to the wills of others. It became the real will.

(ii) It is again pointed out by him that the real will of the individual did not stand alone. It was bound with the real wills of other individuals in society and became the general will. It goes without saying that an individual can grow only in society. So the terms general will and the common life of society, were convertible terms. From this it is seen that full satisfaction of man could not be achieved apart from the satisfaction of the general will.

(iii) Bosanquet further pointed out that the state was the perfect embodiment of the general will. The common life of society depended upon the law and order maintained by the state. Man's life was social. Hence his individual relations were influenced by the common social life. Society was a group of individuals who were united by common general purpose or interest i.e. the ideal of common mind or general will was not a mere fancy. But it was a living reality.

The State : According to Bosanquet institutions were the embodiment of ethical ideas. Every social institution or group was a complicated inter working of the minds of individuals. The totality of the group was reflected in the mind of the individuals Examples of ethical institutions given by him are the family, the group and the state.

In the formation of his theory of state, Bosanquet was influenced by Rousseau's conception of the liberty of the individual the general will of the community and their correlation with each other. The state was the source of all pervading adjustments. In a narrow sense, the state was a political organisation using force. It put its seal of approval on all social efforts which were beneficial to society. In a broader sense the state stood for the general organisation and synthesis of life. It is pointed out here that the state was a necessary factor in a civilised life. It was practically synonymous with society; not an opposing force.

It is known to all that the state is not a mere coercive political organisation as it includes the entire hierarchy of institutions by which life is determined. Thus the state includes the society in it. It is the common substance of the minds of all citizens. The state exists to promote good life. The actions of the state are morally wrong.

According to Bosanquet, "The state is an ethical idea since it is the final working conception of life as a whole." Of all the institutions, it is the supreme institution having a life, mind and will of its own. Its will is the general will. The end of the state is the realisation of the best life as determined by the fundamental logic of the will. Thus the moral purpose is the end of the state. The state promotes good life by maintaining a general system of rights. Rights are claims recognised by the state to the maintenance of conditions to favourable to the best life.

Public and Private Acts : Bosanquet distinguishes the Public Acts from Private Acts. According to him to steal or murder, to lie or to commit personal immorality cannot be public act. A public act which inflicts loss such as war confiscation or repudiation of a debt is wholly different from murder or theft. It is not the act of a private individual. It can be motivated by private malice. It is the act of supreme power. It has ultimate responsibility of protecting the lives of the individuals. This act of the state is subject to criticism.

Punishment : Bosanquet differs from Green with regard to his view on punishment. He agrees with Green that the reformation of the criminal must be the aim of punishment. At the same time he differs from Green in assigning to punishment a positive quality. According to him, there are two regions in the mind of every man viz., conscious and sub-conscious. If his sub-conscious region is affected by an incident or by an accident sooner or later it affects his self also. Hence punishment may affect the conscious will as to bring about a lasting reform in the character of the person punished. Thus it is obvious that the object of punishment is not merely deterrent but also reformatory.

Bosanquet and Green : We have seen already that Bosanquet started with Green and ended in Hegel. There are some differences between the two English political thinkers — Bosanquet and Green. 1. Both stood for the necessity of the state for the realisation of the higher life of man. However, Green was not ready to sacrifice the individual for the sake of state. Bosanquet gave a high place to the state. Further he was prepared to subordinate the individual to the state. 2. Regarding the nature of the state and the proper sphere of state action there is not so much of difference between them. 3. Both believed that the state was an ethical institution. It could not be used directly for promoting morality. 4. Both of them never favoured absolute monarchy. They were true to the English Parliamentary Government and considered it as the very best form of government. 5. Bosanquet and Green differed on the question of resistance to the State. According to Green, the individuals had the right of rebellion may be regarded as unnecessary and unwarranted. 6. Regarding punishment they differed very much. Both of them believed in the deterrent nature of punishment. Bosanquet had positive views than Green in this respect. The former put stress on the psychological aspects of the problem. In other words "the object of punishment is not merely deterrent but also reformatory. 7. Both of them hold different views on the question of war and international morality. Green severely condemned war since it violated the right of every rational being to free life. But in the case of Bonsanquet the acts of the state and the personal acts of individual statesman were different from one another.

Criticism: Many criticisms have been levelled against the philosophy of Dr. Bosanquet. 1. Critics point out that he put too much importance to the institution of state. According to him, the state is the supreme community. Hence it will make the state irresponsible and tyrannical.

2. The identification of the State with society by Bosanquet is wrong. Because the individual was practically merged into the state. It is not conducive to human freedom and progress. Consequently it cannot be defended.

3. The conception of social mind or social will and social organism of Bosanquet has been attacked by many writers. It is very difficult to separate the mind from the body.

4. In the philosophy of Bosanquet there is no scope for an international organisation or international law.

5. The Social will of Bosanquet has been clearly explained. According to Hobhouse, his (Bosanquet's) distinction between the actual and real will is false. Since Bosanquet used the two terms actual and real in the technical sense, his criticism is not proper.

■■

INDEX